HENRY CARTER ADAMS

TAXATION
IN THE
UNITED STATES
1789-1816

Elibron Classics
www.elibron.com

Elibron Classics series.

ISBN 1-4021-9562-1 (paperback)
ISBN 1-4021-1680-2 (hardcover)

This Elibron Classics Replica Edition is an unabridged facsimile of the edition published in 1884 by Johns Hopkins University, Baltimore.

V-VI

TAXATION

IN THE

UNITED STATES

1789-1816

"The *salus populi* should be the prime consideration in regard to all taxes."—*McCulloch.*

"Money is with propriety considered as the vital principle of the body-politic; as that which sustains its life and motion, and enables it to perform its most essential functions." —*Hamilton.*

"Security of property, freedom of industry, and moderation in public expenditure, are the only means by which society can constantly advance in the career of wealth and civilization."—*John Mc Vickar.*

JOHNS HOPKINS UNIVERSITY STUDIES
IN
HISTORICAL AND POLITICAL SCIENCE

HERBERT B. ADAMS, Editor

History is past Politics and Politics present History—*Freeman*

SECOND SERIES

V-VI

TAXATION

IN THE

UNITED STATES

1789-1816

BY HENRY CARTER ADAMS, Ph. D.

BALTIMORE

N. MURRAY, PUBLICATION AGENT, JOHNS HOPKINS UNIVERSITY

MAY AND JUNE, 1884

JOHN MURPHY & CO., PRINTERS,
BALTIMORE.

TAXATION

IN THE

UNITED STATES,

1789-1816.[1]

I.—CUSTOMS DUTIES AND TONNAGE ACTS.

It necessarily follows from the nature of the taxing power that its exercise among free peoples involves much besides securing revenue to States. Questions of general policy, of social purpose, of commercial and industrial interests are found so closely intertwined with questions of tariff, impost, and rates, that a study of the latter group of topics is impossible without entering, to some extent at least, into a consideration of the former. In the history of our own country, this has been especially true since 1816, because of the employment of tax machinery for other than tax purposes; yet even prior to that date, while the protectionist idea from the American standpoint was still in flux, it is found quite difficult to separate revenue questions from current history.

There is one point of marked contrast between the two periods here brought into comparison. Previous to 1816, all

---

[1] The following essay was written in the winter of 1878, while its author was a student at the Johns Hopkins University. During the year 1879, it was translated into German and appeared in the "*Zeitschrift für die gesammte Staatswissenschaft,*" published at Tübingen. The first chapter has been modified, but, in the main, the essay is here presented in its original form. In addition to the facts which it contains, a point of peculiar interest will be found in a new interpretation of the relation which protection held to general politics in 1789.

revenue discussions were largely influenced by considerations of external policy and foreign intercourse, and the workings of revenue laws were, to a considerable degree, affected by the actions of England and France; since the close of the second war with England, however, the politics of the United States have taken their tone and color from questions centering in domestic interests. The treaty of Versailles did not make us a people independent in fact as well as in name. England had no intention of loosening her grasp upon America, or of abandoning, in any essential feature, her traditional colonial policy. Colonial commerce was then of much greater relative importance than at present, and entered more largely into the control of foreign affairs; and the United States, being the first of dependent peoples to deny the claims of the colonial system, found that they had undertaken the solution of a problem demanding radical modification of long-established relations. From one point of view—it may be a narrow point of view—the first twenty-five years of national life may be said to have been devoted to the realization of that independence for which the first great war had been undertaken. In turning our attention, then, to a study of the customs tariff legislation in the United States previous to 1816, we must be prepared for extensive excursions into what at first may appear to be fields of inquiry altogether foreign to financial investigation.

Immediately upon the organization of the House of Representatives, the question of ways and means was introduced as the most pertinent which could engage the attention of Congress. It appears to have been assumed that indirect taxes through duties and imposts should be accepted as the main reliance of the government for revenue, and a plan for the establishment of a system of customs duties was submitted accordingly. This plan received the attention of the House from April 8 to May 17; a formulated bill was then sent to the Senate which, amended by that body and re-amended by a committee of conference, received the approval of the president July 4, 1789. This was the first revenue act under the new government. As finally approved, this law embraced a long list of specific duties, and five classes of goods imposed with *ad valorem* rates. It also contained a short free list, made provision for the repayment of all duties upon goods again exported, and admitted the principle of discrimination in favor of commodities imported in vessels built or owned by citizens of the United States. The details of the act are as follows:

Specific Duties.

Articles taxed.	Rate.	Basis of measure.
Spirits, according to proof	8 to 10 cts	Per gallon.
Wines, according to quality	10 to 18 cts	" "
Beer, Ale, and Porter in Casks	5 cts	" "
Beer, Ale, Porter, and Cider in bottles	20 cts	Per dozen.
Molasses	2½ cts	Per gallon.
Sugars	1 to 3 cts	Per pound.
Teas, from China in American vessels	6 to 20 cts	" "
Teas, from Europe in American vessels	8 to 26 cts	" "
Teas imported in any other manner	15 to 45 cts	" "
Candles of wax or spermaceti	6 cts	" "
Tallow candles and soap	2 cts	" "
Cheese	4 cts	" "
Boots	50 cts	Per pair.
Shoes of leather	7 cts	" "
Shoes of silk	10 cts	" "
Cables and tarred cordage	75 cts	Per 112 pounds.
Untarred cordage	90 cts	" " "
Twine and packthread	$2.00	" " "
Unwrought steel	56 cts	" " "
Nails and spikes	1 ct	Per pound.
Manufactured tobacco	6 cts	" "
Snuff	10 cts	" "
Indigo	16 cts	" "
Hemp	60 cts	Per 112 pounds.
Cotton	3 cts	Per pound.
Wool and cotton cards	50 cts	Per dozen.
Coal	2 cts	Per bushel.
Pickled fish	75 cts	Per barrel.
Dried fish	50 cts	Per quintal.
Salt	6 cts	Per bushel.
Coffee	2½ cts	Per pound.
Cocoa	1 ct	" "

Ad Valorem Duties.

Goods paying ten per cent; Glass of all kinds except black quart bottles; all china, stone and earthen-ware; gunpowder; paints ground in oil; shoe and knee buckles; lace and leaf of gold and silver.

Goods paying seven and a half per cent; Blank books; writing, printing, or wrapping paper; paper hangings and pasteboard; cabinet-ware, buttons, saddles, gloves of leather, fur, wool, or beaver hats, millinery goods, ready-made clothing; leather, castings of iron, or iron slit and rolled, anchors, and all wrought tin or pewter ware; brushes, walking canes, and whips.

Carriages or parts thereof were to pay fifteen per cent.; goods (other than teas) from India or China, not brought in American ships, were imposed with twelve and one-half per cent. All unspecified importations were charged with a tax of five per cent. of their value at time and place of importation. The free list included saltpetre, tin in pigs, tin plates, lead, old pewter, brass, iron and brass wire, copper in plates, wool, cotton, dyeing woods and dyeing drugs, raw hides, beaver, and all other furs, and deer skins. From the rates imposed as above stated, a discount of ten per cent. was allowed on such goods as should be imported in vessels owned in America, and a drawback of all duties paid (ten per cent. being retained for expenses incurred) on goods which, within twelve months, should be exported to some foreign country.

Although this first law was introduced as a temporary measure, it is yet the center of deeper historical interest than any other revenue act that comes under consideration in this essay; for it not only presents questions that are unsettled, but suggests also a line of study bearing directly upon the theory of historical development in the United States. The preamble of the law is as follows: "Whereas it is necessary for the support of the government, for the discharge of the debts of the United States, and the encouragement and protection of manufactures, that duties be laid on goods, wares and merchandise imported," &c. The law of 1790, which increased duties about two and one-half per cent., laid no especial stress upon the encouragement of manufactures, although the revenue element was brought into greater prominence, making the duties levied co-existent with the debts for which they were imposed. Now there are two questions that suggest themselves respecting the "encouragement and protection" clause of this first law. The one asks how far the proclaimed purpose of this act was realized and to what extent the development of industries in the United States previous to 1816 is traceable to the fostering care of the government. This question, as also criticisms upon the financial workings of the revenue system as a whole, will claim attention in the last chapter of this essay. The second question, and the one that presents itself for immediate consideration, leads to the necessity of studying anew the meaning of this word protection, the reason for its appearance in the first revenue act, and the development of the protective idea up to 1816. At this latter date, all will admit that the protective idea had grown into a perfect and independent policy, with its party of adherents and opponents, and that it has so remained till the present day; but the interpretations respecting the period covered by the present study are not altogether harmonious. The question, then, is concerning the germ of the "American System" of protection and the conditions out of which it was developed. Our purpose is to learn, if possible, how far political events, on the one hand, and industrial ideas, on the other, are responsible for the shape which protection finally took.

Respecting the first step in the prosecution of such an inquiry, there is no cause for hesitation. To weigh the relative importance of industrial and political considerations in giving shape to the American protective system, one must first learn the industrial condition of the United States in 1789, and grasp intelligently those combinations of interests and purposes that go to make up a political policy. Our first task, then, consists in a study of industrial conditions.

Industrial Interests of the United States in 1789.

The population of the colonies during the Revolutionary war had been much overestimated, and the enumeration in 1790 was the source of disappointment to the American people. The census returns were as follows:

White males of sixteen and upwards	813,298
White males under sixteen	802,327
White females	1,556,839
All other persons (free blacks)	59,466
Slaves	697,879
Total number of inhabitants	3,929,827

This classification, adopted to determine Congressional representation, is of no direct importance for the purpose in hand, but, by applying the averages which statisticians of that day accepted as correct, the total population included in the so-called laboring class may be estimated at 3,049,000. This number embraced all not engaged in professional and commercial pursuits, as also many not of the laboring age. The kind of industries to which this labor was applied can only be ascertained from the political speeches, the addresses, and essays of the day.

The industry which received by far the greatest attention in the United States was agriculture. Benjamin Franklin in 1789, speaking of New England, said, "Calculations carefully made do not raise the portion of property or the number of men employed in manufactures, fisheries, navigation, and trade to one-eighth of the property and people occupied by agriculture even in that commercial quarter."[1] Tench Coxe,

[1] Address before the "Society for Political Enquirers" of Philadelphia, May 11, 1789.

the same year, estimated that nine-tenths of the population of the United States were engaged in agricultural pursuits, and the debates of the first Congress indicate that this fact was perfectly recognized by the statesmen of 1789.[1]

The products to which this agricultural labor was applied may be grouped under the three following classes: (*a*) Vegetable food-products, wheat, corn, rice, potatoes, etc.; (*b*) Products of animal life, such as beef, mutton, pork, hides, wool, butter, lard; (*c*) Products of the soil other than foods, such as tobacco, cotton, indigo, hemp, timber.

With regard to the products raised at this time, the territory of the United States may be divided into four districts: New England and part of New York comprised the first; from the central part of New York to the southern boundary of Pennsylvania, the second; Maryland and Virginia, the third; and the remaining Southern States, the fourth. The New England district was chiefly devoted to the raising of agricultural products of the second class. "In the Eastern States, cattle are very numerous and generally large. Cheese is abundant. No European State can exceed the United States in the article of salt provision. Sheep are bred in all parts of the country, but in New England they form one of the greatest objects of the farmer's care and one of the surest sources of profit."[2] The wheat-growing territory lay in the second district. In 1789 Pennsylvania exported two million and New York, one million bushels of that staple. In the debates during the convention of 1787, Mr. Pinckney spoke of the flour trade of Pennsylvania and New Jersey.[3] Virginia and Maryland also exported large quantities of wheat, but the chief source of wealth to this third agricultural district was found in the growing of tobacco. Before the war, those

---

[1] Coxe, View of the United States, p. 6.

[2] Most of these facts are taken from Coxe's View of the United States, ch. vi, "For the information of migrators from foreign countries."

[3] Wednesday, Aug. 29.

States exported annually between eighty and ninety thousand hogsheads of tobacco. The States lying yet farther south, besides raising some tobacco, furnished large quantities of rice and indigo. The South Carolina crop of rice in 1789 was sixty millions of pounds. Cotton had not yet come to be a staple for the Southern States, but was considered as a commodity for which there might arise a demand. In regard to mineral resources it was known that all the States but Delaware contained iron, and it was supposed that Virginia was exceedingly rich in metals of all kinds.

That industry which, in the United States, stood second in importance to agriculture was commerce. It is, however, very difficult to procure specific knowledge respecting ships and seamen for the period now under consideration. For the year ending September, 1790, American vessels, engaged in the foreign trade, amounted to 365,093 tons, while American coasting and fishing vessels amounted to 149,433 tons.[1] In the year 1789, out of eighty-nine foreign ships in the ports of China, fifteen bore the American flag, though it is quite probable that some of these represented English capital.[2] These figures present, however inadequately, some idea of the extent of American commerce, but even these facts were not known to the members of the first Congress. They knew in general that New England owned the greater part of domestic shipping, and that her seamen were endeavoring to compete with England in the carrying trade of America, but, as will appear later, the tonnage-bill and those clauses of the tariff-bill which discriminated against foreign vessels, received approbation as political rather than as economic measures.

Manufactures, in 1789, were of comparatively slight importance, being restricted for the most part to articles which may be considered as one step removed from raw material, as for example, flour made from wheat, or snuff from tobacco.

---

[1] Compare Pitkin's Commerce of the United States, ch. xi.

[2] McPherson's Annals of Commerce, p. 195.

To go beyond this would have required capital and skill, neither of which the young States possessed. The only exception to this was the industry of ship-building. Better and cheaper ships could be built in the United States than in Europe. The cost of an oak vessel in Massachusetts was about twenty-four Mexican dollars per ton, while live oak and American cedar could be made for thirty-six or thirty-eight dollars per ton. A fir vessel on the Baltic cost thirty-five dollars, while an oak ship in England, Holland, or France cost fifty or sixty dollars per ton.[1] American ships had been the great manufactures for exportation. "For nicety of workmanship the palm was awarded to Philadelphia, but nowhere could they be built so cheaply as at Boston. More than one-third of the tonnage employed in British commerce, before the war, was of American construction."[2]

The manufacture of rum in New England and of beer in Pennsylvania was also very extensive; in case of the latter the only hindrance was lack of black quart bottles. This fact seems to have been known in Congress, as appears from the exemption of such bottles from the ten per cent. duty imposed upon other kinds of glass ware. Drying fish was also an extensive business in the Eastern States, this product being exchanged with the West Indies for molasses. There was no steam mill on the continent, the force of wind, water, and animals being relied upon for such power as the industries required. In general, these facts were well known to the members of the first Congress, and they recognized also—what some of their critics fail to recognize—that the treaty of Versailles, which had gained for them political independence, had set them outside the course of English commerce and materially disturbed the old trade relations.

The significance of these industrial facts will appear more distinctly as we proceed in our study.

---

[1] Coxe's View of the United States, p. 100.

[2] Bancroft's History of the Constitution of the United States, I., p. 63.

Political Origin of Protection.

Turning now to a consideration of the political creed of the American people, one quickly perceives that its roots run far back into colonial conditions and that its temporary expression in 1789 was shaped by peculiar foreign relations. What then, we must inquire, were the foreign relations of the newly established Federal government?

When the first Congress convened, definite treaties between the United States and foreign powers were confined to a treaty of "Peace" with Great Britain; of "Amity and Commerce" with France, Prussia, Sweden, and the Netherlands; and of "Peace and Friendship" with Morocco. Commercial intercourse with all other countries was according to the common law of nations, modified by the internal regulations of each particular country. The "Amity and Commerce" treaties were intended to be in harmony with principles of reciprocity. They provided that free ships should make free goods and persons, except persons actually in the service of the enemy; and freedom of trade was also allowed to each contracting nation with the enemy of another nation. The historical significance of the international relations thus disclosed lies in the fact that the commercial possibilities of the United States were neither restricted nor yet guaranteed to any great degree by treaty-law, but were dependent rather upon the temporary policies of foreign powers. This possibility of dependence, and the disposition on the part of European peoples to exercise control over American trade, throws much light upon those clauses of the first tariff law which discriminated in favor of domestic shipping, and explains also the rapid growth of American neutral commerce.

Of especial importance to the United States was the attitude of England in respect to matters of trade. Habit, similarity in the mode of living, and the long credit which English merchants were willing to give, rendered trade with Great Britain of more importance than with all other nations. For the year ending September, 1790, of twenty millions of exports to thirteen foreign countries, nine millions went to the dominions of Great Britain; yet the only clause contained in the treaty with that nation relating to commerce was the one which proclaimed the navigation of the Mississippi open to both nations. To understand the conditions under which this trade took place, it will be necessary to notice the commercial policy of England and the effort which she made to apply it to the American States at the close of the Revolutionary War. The purpose of England was to maintain the people of this country in colonial dependence, and her foreign policy still found its theoretical basis in the old system of Mercantilism. The means by which this was to be carried out were very simple, consisting simply in requiring that all goods, so far as England could control them, should be carried in British ships. According to this system, as stated by one connected with its application at the time, "the only use of colonies was the monopoly of their carrying trade and consumption. . . . . . Our late war has been for the exclusive trade of America, and our enormous debt has been incurred for that object." The object of the war had not been relinquished by England when the Colonies were granted their political freedom, and it now became the purpose of Great Britain to secure through navigation acts what she had lost at arms. In 1783, Mr. Pitt introduced into Parliament a bill for the regulation of commerce between the two countries which, had it passed, would have laid the foundation of lasting friendship; but which "had it passed," said Lord Sheffield, "would have undermined the whole naval power of Great Britain." After the failure of this bill the King and council were granted power to regulate commerce with the American States. The first order under this grant was on the 26th of December, an order not radically changed until 1794. According to the regulations imposed, importations of any un-manufactured goods, the growth or product of any of the United States of America, were permitted subject to the payment of common duties, "if imported by British subjects, in British ships." The forest and agricultural products, and live stock of America, could be exported to the West Indies in British bottoms only, while the rum, sugar, molasses, and other products of those islands, could only be carried to the States in ships built and owned by British subjects.

It was by such regulations that England thought to retain the exclusive trade of America. To meet this policy and secure emancipation from its assuming tyranny, was one of the most powerful arguments which led the States to vest Congress with the power to regulate commerce. England denied that any commercial treaty whatever was necessary with the United States. "It is impossible," said Lord Sheffield, "to name any material advantage the American States will or can give us more than what we, of course, shall have." This was not an opinion carelessly made, but based upon a careful survey of the kind of goods which the United States would consume and which England could supply; and, considering the industrial position of England and the amount of her accumulated capital, which allowed goods to be sold upon long credit, it must be recognized that this position of the British ministry was well taken, for it lay in their power to control the trade of this country without granting a single privilege. The exercise of such a policy appeared to the Americans unjust and harmful to their national interests, and they expected that the newly formed government, centralized to such a degree that, in many quarters, it was occasion of grave solicitude, would adopt measures adequate to secure protection from its evil consequences.

It has, as it appears to me, been carelessly assumed by a certain class of writers that it would have been well for the United States to have accepted the situation and rested content with such trade as England would have permitted. But there are certain points to be noticed in connection with this claim. The political nationality of America was dependent upon the emancipation of her industries from the commercial regulations of England. Without this, nationality was an empty name. No new purpose was infused into public sentiment which led members of the first Congress to resist the mercantile system above described, for it was just this which America had been resisting for more than a century. The method of coercion adopted by England had alone been changed. It was a demand for emancipation from England's colonial policy that first led to hostilities against the mother country; it was the same purpose that led to continued resistance. But more than this, there was, commercially considered, no possibility for freedom of trade. The highest benefits of freedom of exchange are only procurable when there is an open market for sale as well as for purchase, but, at this time, the conditions of trade were such that competition was confined to sellers, buyers being comparatively free from its regulating potency. Trade was largely carried on by men called "factors," and the condition of American producers under the navigation acts was somewhat analogous to that which would arise should a State legislature pass a law requiring all people living in the country to deal, both in selling and buying, with certain privileged pedlers.

It was out of such foreign relations as we have described that the political purpose of 1789 arose, and it must be confessed that they indicate a somewhat complicated state of affairs. In general one may say that the controlling tendency of public sentiment from 1789 to 1816 was toward a stronger government, although the line described presents many deviations from direct approach. These deviations are somewhat difficult to follow because of frequent interchange in cause and effect. What at one time must be regarded as the consequence of experienced evils arising out of weakness in the central authority, at another becomes the conscious purpose of the administration. Thus, subsequently to 1783, the futile effort of the various States to avoid independently the commercial purposes of Great Britain gave birth to a desire for a power national in reality as well as in name, and was influential in securing from the American people a reluctant consent to the new constitution. During these years one may correctly say that the idea of a strong government was a resultant and not a causal factor in public life.

But by the year 1790, adequate central authority had been granted, and the men instrumental in securing it had been entrusted with the task of forming and administering a public policy. The controlling idea now came to be that of strong government, and all subordinate questions were moulded so as to support this one purpose. One cannot, therefore, judge correctly of the early financial policy of the United States, or, indeed, of any other measure which was made to contribute to the realization of a strong government, independently of this fact.

In 1801, when the Republicans came into power, the logic of action was again changed. The avowed purpose of the victorious party was to check the tendency toward centralization, but necessity was stronger than purpose and very little was done to redeem the pledges which the opponents of the Hamiltonian system had given during the controversy which brought them to office. The government drifted until 1807, when foreign affairs became so threatening as to throw the thought of the country again in upon itself. The commerce of the country, which up to this time had been unprecedentedly prosperous, was destroyed, and energy and capital were turned into the channel of manufactures. There was then a revival of that spirit of nationality which gave birth to the war party and again reversed the order of the syllogism to which public action conformed. Between this period of nationality, however, and the one that was observed to direct public opinion under the Federalist administration, there is one point of marked contrast. Agriculture was the important industry in both periods; but, in the former instance, it was commerce that drew to itself such labor and capital as could be freed from the soil, and claimed the greater attention of the legislature. In the second period, manufactures are observed to have usurped the position in public estimation formerly occupied by trade. A commercial war is always propitious for the establishment of new industries, and in the present case there was developed an intense desire to maintain by law, after the cessation of hostilities, those conditions which secured to industries control over the home market. Then for the first time was it that protection as an independent industrial system forced its way into the history of the United States. The "American System" of protection took its rise out of the struggle of contradictory purposes which the record of the first twenty-five years of national existence discloses,—a system which, looked at in its inception and growth, must be regarded as the formulated purpose of this people to throw off completely the yoke of colonial dependence. The theory of interpretation, therefore, which alone can give unity to this first period of revenue history is that the protective purpose was a subordinate part of a permanent and a strong political purpose, and he who undertakes to explain it from the standpoint of trade interests alone can never hope to touch bottom.

Early Sentiments Respecting Commerce.

One could hardly expect that a mere statement of this theory of interpretation would procure its immediate acceptance, although it will, I apprehend, be quite generally acceded to if the first tariff law of 1789 and the report upon manufactures by Hamilton in 1791 can be brought into harmony with its claims. Subsequent State papers and revenue acts, even upon their face, support rather than contradict the theory. The real question at issue, then, has reference to the sentiment and the purpose which determined these first revenue laws.

Some light may be thrown upon the question by discovering the opinions of eminent statesmen of this period with respect to trade and commerce. Inferential testimony may be found in the quick acceptance on this side of the water of the doctrines of Adam Smith. It may be regarded as at least a curious coincidence that the "Wealth of Nations" and the Declaration of Independence were presented to the world during the course of the same year. This work of the great Scotchman has probably exerted more influence in forming the character of the Nineteenth Century than any other one book published. It served as the intellectual basis for the establishment of a system of industrial freedom. The mental process which led to its conception was altogether analogous to that which resulted in the declaration "That these United Colonies are, and of right ought to be, Free and Independent States." Its reasoning was hurled against that system of commercial usurpation which gave tone to the entire political life of the Eighteenth century, and it was the yoke of this same system resting upon the American Colonies that caused them passionately to sever all bonds uniting them to the country of their ancestry.

It would be both interesting and instructive to trace the influence exerted by the writings of Adam Smith upon the early development of this country. In looking over the speeches, pamphlets and letters of the day, one finds frequent allusions to the "Wealth of Nations," showing that it was a work well known and quite generally endorsed. For example, in a private letter written by Fisher Ames while a member of Congress, in speaking of Mr. Madison, we find the following: "He adopts maxims as he finds them in books. . . . One of his first speeches in regard to protecting commerce was taken out of Smith's Wealth of Nations."[1] Or again, if Mr. Gallatin be accepted as authority, the framers of the Constitution had in mind certain distinctions made by Adam Smith when they adopted into that instrument the words "capitation, direct, and indirect tax." After defining these terms as he understood them, Mr. Gallatin adds: "It

[1] Letter to Minot, May 29, 1789.

may not be improper to corroborate it [this is his interpretation of the phrases] by quoting the author from whom the idea seems to have been borrowed," and he then proceeds to quote from the second chapter of the fifth book of the "Wealth of Nations."[1] Monroe, in a letter to Jefferson, cited "a Mr. Smith on the Wealth of Nations" as having written "that the doctrine of the balance of trade is a chimera,"[2] and if one desire the source from which Hamilton drew the anti-physiocratic argument in his report upon manufactures, he will find it in the Wealth of Nations.[3]

These facts are cited as proof that our early statesmen knew and appreciated the worth of Adam Smith's writings. This fact is not at all peculiar when we recognize the position held by the American States in reference to the old colonial system. Many of these men regarded Adam Smith as one who had reduced to literary form their own political beliefs. His disciples in England were their friends, and they desired, so far as possible, to realize in this new land his ideal of commercial freedom. Their appreciation of this work shows the philosophical purpose of their political endeavors, and common fairness in writing history requires that their actions be brought into harmony with this purpose, or that the reasons for departing from it be pointed out.

We are not, however, confined to inferential testimony. It certainly stands for something that in the Declaration of Independence itself one finds a demand for unshackled commerce. In that long list of indictments against George III. there stood this charge, that, under the guise of "pretended legis-

---

[1] Sketch of United States in 1796, p. 12. Old edition. By Albert Gallatin.

[2] Monroe to Jefferson, June 16, 1785, MS. See Bancroft, History of the Constitution, vol. I., p. 195.

[3] I confess I am not fully satisfied as to the connection here suggested or the meaning of the quotation marks inserted in the report. But that some connection exists, may be seen by comparing the Report with Book IV., ch. 9, of Smith's Wealth of Nations.

lation," he had cut off "trade with all parts of the world." It must be remembered that this was before the rise of that doctrine of protection which depreciates profits arising from commerce, and which over-estimates the productivity of labor devoted to manufactures; and, since this country had no thought of colonies for herself and so could not have regarded protection from the European point of view, this charge must be interpreted as a demand for freedom of trade.[1] It is also a very significant fact that the Constitution declares against restrictions upon trade between the various States,—a provision in our organic law which has probably been more potent than any other in maintaining natural integrity and unity upon American soil.

The sound judgment which Mr. Bancroft has shown as a student of American history will hardly be denied, and it is with especial pleasure that his language may be quoted in support of the position here taken. In speaking of the relations existing between this country and Great Britain in 1783, he says:[2] "In America there existed as yet no system of restrictions; and congress had not power to protect shipping or establish a custom house. The States as dependencies had been so severely and so wantonly cramped by British navigation acts and for more than a century had so steadily resisted them, that the desire of absolute freedom of commerce had become a part of their nature. The American commissioners were very much pleased with the trade bill of Pitt, and with the principles expressed in its preamble; the debates upon it in parliament awakened their distrust. Their choice and their offer was mutual, unconditional free trade, but, however

---

[1] The question suggested by this comparison is a most interesting one. There is an essential difference in theory between that protection which formed a part of the Mercantile or Colonial system and that which now controls States, and which may properly be termed internal protection. A comparison of these two systems would form a most instructive economic monograph.

[2] History of the Constitution of the United States, Vol. I., p. 64.

narrow might be the limits which England should impose, they were resolved to insist on like for like." After stating somewhat fully the interests in controversy, he continues: "Such was the issue between the ancient nation which falsely and foolishly and mischievously believed that its superiority in commerce was due to artificial legislation, and a young people which solicited free trade." In a diplomatic conversation that occurred between Mr. Pitt and John Adams two years later, 1785, there is a question and reply very significant for our present purpose which I venture to paraphrase as follows. Referring to a treaty of commerce, Mr. Pitt asked: "What are the lowest terms which will be satisfactory to America?" To this inquiry Mr. Adams replied diplomatically, pointed out his want of power to give a final answer to such a question, then ventured to state what, in his opinion, would secure to England "the friendship of the United States and the essence of their trade." To this he added: "The most judicious men in America have been long balancing in their mind the advantages and disadvantages of a commerce entirely free on the one side, and a navigation act on the other. The present time is a critical one. The late intelligencies from all parts of America concur with the navigation act of Massachusetts in proving which way the balance begins to incline, and, in my opinion, the issue will be decided by the conduct of this country; indeed, it now lies in your power to decide it. But the more Americans reflect upon the great advantages which might be derived from a navigation act, the more attached will they become to that system." Later in the conversation, Pitt asked if the Americans could think hard of the English for encouraging their own shipwrights, their manufacturers of ships, and their own whale fishery. "By no means," said Mr. Adams, "but it appears unaccountable to the people of America, that this country [England] should sacrifice the general interest of the nation to the private interest of a few individuals interested in the manufacture of ships and in the whale fishery, so far as to refuse these remittances from

America, in payment of debts, and for manufactures which would employ so many more people, augment the revenue so considerably, as well as the national wealth, which would, even in other ways, so much augment the shipping of the nation. It is looked upon in America as reconciling yourself to a diminution of your own shipping and seamen, in a great degree, for the sake of diminishing ours in a small one, besides keeping many of your manufacturers out of employ, who would otherwise have enough to do. This is contrary to the maxim [a maxim which Pitt had admitted] that one nation should not hurt itself for the sake of hurting another, nor take measures to deprive another of any advantage, without benefiting itself."[1] This conversation took place upon the 24th of August. Nine days after, in a letter to Governor Bowdoin, John Adams wrote: "The Massachusetts has often been wise and able; but she never took a deeper measure than her late navigation act. I hope she will persist in it even though she should be alone." He hoped that by persistence in restriction America would secure ultimate freedom. In a letter to Jefferson, his view upon restrictions and the use to be made of them is expressed in this language. "I should be sorry to adopt a monopoly, but driven to the necessity of it, I should not do things by halves. If monopolies and exclusions are the only arms of defence against monopolies and exclusions, I would venture upon them without fear of offending Dean Tucker or the ghost of Doctor Quesnay."[2]

The sentiments of John Adams as here expressed properly represent the views of the early American statesmen, and his

---

[1] Letter from Adams to Jay, August 25, 1785.

[2] Dean Tucker was an English writer who advocated separation from the colonies and freedom of intercourse, claiming that every substantial advantage could, in that manner, be retained. See, for example, "Four tracts on Political and Commercial subjects," 1770, pp. 202 to 224; being part of Tract IV., "The Interest of Great Britain Set Forth in Regard to her Colonies." Doctor Quesnay was the founder of a school of Economists in France, that advocated commercial freedom. His first important work, "Tableau Économique," appeared in 1758.

characterization of the birth of restrictive ideas among the people is one that will stand the test of a most exhaustive study. It was the impetus of this sentiment that cemented the independent States into a central government and carried to success the establishment of the first revenue law. The restrictions in this law were counter-restrictions, and the protection it afforded was primarily protection against that system of commercial usurpation which England had undertaken to enforce.[1] Here is presented the first phase of that permanent policy which afterwards came to be known as the "American System." It seems never to have occurred to some who attempt to interpret this law, that words have historic meanings and cannot safely be wrested from the settings in which they were presented; such writers also fail to recognize that to demand protection against open competition with foreign producers calls for a radically different mental attitude from that assumed by those who voted for the first revenue act. The demand for protection in this instance, as well as the grant of protection, was indissolubly bound up with the political purpose of that day, and may, I think, be most easily understood, if confined to the wish of the American people for participation in the carrying trade of the world.

But, it may be asked, suppose this be admitted so far as "protection" is concerned, can the phrase "encouragement of manufactures" found in the preamble to the law of 1789 be explained in the same manner? This phrase appears to have presented no very definite idea to the minds of those who early made use of it, although so far as form is concerned, there is here found something quite analogous to protection from competition for the sake of the industry. At its incep-

---

[1] "The Americans" said Mr. Adams to Mr. Pitt, "think that their exclusion from your West India Islands, the refusal of their ships and oils and other things, and their exclusion from your colonies on the continent and Newfoundland, discover a jealousy of their naval power, and a fixed system of policy to prevent the growth of it; and this is an idea that they cannot bear."

tion, however, this too was based upon a deep political purpose. The germ of this desire for manufactures, even though they must be artificially fostered, is found in the determination of the American people to be independent of England, first, because they were denied political rights, but afterwards, because they were refused open markets for American produce. This desire appeared very early and found its expression in public meetings, in resolutions, and in inter-colonial agreements against the consumption of foreign productions. Perhaps the manifestation of this spirit in Georgia is as interesting and instructive as any that may be presented.[1] In 1775, the Provincial Assembly passed resolutions refusing to use imported goods. Georgia had been omitted from the application of the "bill restraining trade," but "looked upon this exception rather as an insult than a favor." The sentiment of these resolutions portrays no appreciation whatever of the restrictive policy as a means of effecting the establishment of manufactures. They may be more properly characterized in the language of the present, as showing the determined purpose of "Boycotting" not only the English merchants, but any home dealer or American colony that should hold intercourse with England before certain alleged grievances should be redressed. This also was the purpose of the agreement between the merchants of Boston, New York, and Philadelphia in 1768.[2] Self-dependence having been suggested in this manner, it became the fashion for public men to appear in home-spun suits and to praise any endeavor to establish home industries; and it is not at all strange that they who were benefited by the creation of this home-demand should press the desirability of maintaining these self-imposed restrictions by legal enactment. It was in this manner that, through the lapse of years, what at its inception was a mere political purpose grew into an established industrial theory. The

[1] Stevens' History of Georgia, Vol. II., p. 111.
[2] Watson's Annals of Philadelphia, Vol. II., p. 272.

important point, however, for us to notice is, that the form of the argument then used was entirely different from that employed now by those who desire to persuade men to adopt the same measures. The argument then regarded as convincing was: 'The sure way to establish nationality is to exclude foreign products;' now, on the other hand, we hear: 'The sure way to become rich is to exclude foreign products.'

How far toward the acceptance of this fully developed idea of protection public sentiment had arrived in 1789, is a question most difficult to answer. The evidence upon which it is necessary to rely is found in the previous action of the States, and in the discussions that attended the enactment of the first law. So far as the Navigation acts of the several States are concerned, they were passed as temporary measures looking toward the granting of larger powers to the central government, and so are of comparatively slight importance; but besides these there are certain tariff acts that show somewhat clearer ideas of protection for the sake of the industry. Thus, in the year 1785, the State of Rhode Island raised her import duties from five to twenty per cent., for the purpose, as the preamble stated, of encouraging manufacture within this State of the United States.[1] Pennsylvania also passed an act after six months' deliberation to "protect the manufacturers."[2] There appears to be no good reason for believing that these laws did not mean what they state, and we are therefore compelled to admit that, in these localities, a foreshadowing of the modern restrictive system is discoverable. The only question is, how far did these ideas permeate the entire country, and at what point in their development did they become general.

With regard to the debates in the first Congress it appears to me that they have been sadly misapprehended.[3] That one

---

[1] Arnold's History of Rhode Island, Vol. II., p. 513.

[2] Bancroft, History of Constitution, Vol. I., p. 187.

[3] Mr. Benton's interpretation of these discussions is in harmony with the one here presented. See note in "Abridgments of Debates," Vol. I., p. 84.

may find here expressions contradicting all liberality of sentiment, that after a few days the deliberations of this first Congress degenerated into "a grand grab struggle between interests and sections," and that there was then illustrated as clearly as ever since the folly of endeavoring to secure the benefits of protection to all interests, is not denied; but, notwithstanding this, it is urged that the conscious formulation of a protective system except as a subordinate part of a political purpose, can be found only in a period much later than 1789. Here again the environment of the discussion and an appreciation of what was not said is essential for a rational interpretation.

Thus, in the first place, consider the magnitude of the question at issue in this first debate, and the solicitude with which the leading statesmen must have regarded the course of the discussion. The fact that the Constitution had been adopted, or rather that consent to a document had been forced from a reluctant people, by no means guaranteed to this country a stable Government. The question at issue was: Is this document a piece of waste paper, or does it contain the organic law of a self-governing people? The answer was simple: If revenue can be secured upon the basis of some law which goes forth from Congress with practical harmony of sentiment, the new State will stand forth a fact; without a law thus presented, the labor of years will prove abortive. It is the magnitude of the question at issue that explains that courtesy and willingness to make concessions on the part of the leader of the House, a willingness that would hardly have appeared had the permanency of the government been ensured. The history of this discussion does not seem difficult to understand. Mr. Madison, recognizing the importance of funds, introduced, immediately upon the organization of the House, resolutions to the effect that the five per cent. impost act of 1783 should be accepted as a model after which to shape a temporary law. Mr. Boudinot followed the presentation of these innocent resolutions, saying that, as he understood it, the proposed law would be but a temporary arrangement "calculated to embrace the spring importations," and added a motion" that the blanks be filled up in the manner they were recommended to be charged by Congress in 1783. Mr. White wished more time to think of the matter, and Mr. Madison said, "certainly," and seconded the motion that the committee rise. Upon the next day, Mr. Lawrence (afterward advocate for protection on beer) expressed his approval of the resolutions, but suggested that it would be less confusing "to lay a duty at a certain rate per cent. on the value of all articles without attempting an enumeration of any." He was followed by Mr. Fitzsimmons of Pennsylvania, who deprecated a temporary system and proposed that the matter be undertaken thoroughly, and that the revenue law be shaped for protective purposes. After two speeches opposed to this suggestion, Mr. Hartly of the same State arose and presented a set argument for protection. It was at this juncture that Mr. Madison made that speech so frequently quoted, but as frequently misinterpreted, in which he said: "I own myself the friend of a very free system of commerce." A polemical historian says of him in the spirit of criticism: "He was one of those who believe that a doctrine can be true and its application unwise." He who would understand this speech must appreciate Mr. Madison's position. He was a member of a deliberative body that had no precedents whatever. No vote had as yet been taken in the House indicating how party-lines might form, and he could count on no following; nor had he any sure way of forecasting public sentiment. He conceived that the success of the new Constitution depended upon presenting to the country a revenue law to which all members of Congress should be equally committed. What would have been the result if Mr. Madison had been less timid, it is of course useless at present to conjecture, but the fact seems to be, that, rather than permit faction lines to be drawn before ways and means could be provided for the new government, he was willing to make great concessions, and he did make the concession of allowing the debates to proceed upon the assumption of protection rather than run the risk of alienating the Pennsylvania delegation.[1] If this theory of the debates be the true one, it follows that the phrase "encouragement and protection of manufactures," in the preamble, is the price paid for substantial harmony in presenting this first revenue act to the country,—a compromise the more readily acceded to because protection was then regarded by all as but an incident to the securing of revenue, and, contrary to the wish of the protectionist advocates, the law was declared a temporary measure.

But what shall be said of the Hamilton report upon manufactures? Does not this show the presence of industrial protection as an independent, aggressive factor? It is assumed that the facts of this report are well known, and we are therefore excused from a re-statement of them. Nor is it of present importance that this report is, in many of its parts, illogical and contrary to sound economic doctrine, for we are concerned alone with its historical interpretation.

Attention has been already called to the fact that the desire for a strong government, which, prior to 1789, sprang spontaneously from the experienced evils of executive weakness, came to be the controlling motive of the first administration under the new Constitution, and the true significance of this report upon manufactures can only be discerned in the light of this fact. Many measures had been already taken to induce coherency in the system before the appearance of this paper. A National Bank had been established, the refunding scheme set on foot, assumption of State debts pressed to acceptance, and steps taken towards providing for national coinage. All these measures were under the guidance of one very simple definite purpose which gave direction to the

---

[1] It is claimed that the Morrill tariff was the price paid by the Republican leaders for the adherence of Pennsylvania to the party in 1861. Compare Sumner's "Protection in the United States," p. 56.

thought of the Federal party, and this purpose was to secure executive centralization and to build up a sentiment of nationality. This report upon manufactures must be viewed in the same light and take its place by the side of these other measures; indeed, it cannot be separated and treated as an isolated State paper without doing violence to plain rules of historical interpretation. It seems legitimate, therefore, to conclude that the protectionist sentiment which gave rise to this report, as well as that in the community to which it appealed, was very far from being a sentiment merely industrial in character or resting wholly on an industrial basis; indeed, one is warranted in saying that it proves the total subordination of the industrial to the political problem. Can one think that Bismarck honestly believes that his newly-enacted corn laws will enrich the people of Germany? What he wants is nationality at any cost. This is what the leaders of the Federal party wanted in 1791, and it is this political purpose, rather than any industrial theory, that is the key to the real meaning of Hamilton's report upon manufactures. This interpretation harmonizes perfectly with what Hamilton avowed as his purpose, "to let the thirteen states, bound together in a great indissoluble union, concur in erecting one great system superior to the control of transatlantic force or influences, and able to dictate the connection between the old and new world."

Another fact, significant as pointing toward this same theory of interpretation, is found in the further development of the general financial policy of the government. The average rate of duties imposed by the law of 1792, which is said to realize the purpose of the Hamilton report, was but thirteen and one-half per cent., and this extension was justified by the need of revenue to protect the frontiers. The two and one-half per cent. addition to the list of un-specified articles, bringing the rate up to seven and one-half per cent., was limited by the law to two years, when it was supposed the exigency would have passed. Until the expiration of these two years, no new tariff act was presented, and, after that, there were no decided changes of a protective character. But the point of importance for us is, that the rate of customs had by no means reached the limit which experience has shown to be the highest revenue rate; yet, notwithstanding this, there was introduced and developed by this Federal party (supposed to be a party adopting protective theories) a general system of internal duties. Had the rate upon customs reached twenty or twenty-five per cent., this resort to excise could be explained even upon the assumption of protection, but the introduction of other taxes while customs rates were far below the revenue standard, shows that there was no understanding, or at least no appreciation of a fully developed system of protection in the control of the treasury department. And further, it must be remembered that excise duties, when placed on articles with which foreign articles compete, counteract the protective force of the customs tariff, and this was the case so far as beer and spirits were concerned. It seems, therefore, proper to say, without pressing the statement too far, that the subsequent development of treasury-management does not show such strict adherence to the principles of the report upon manufactures as to warrant one in reading from it the formulated opinion of the country. It afterwards became a State paper of importance, when the reputation of its author could be used to bolster up a system which had developed so far as to invite criticism; but, at the time of its appearance, it is very doubtful if its full significance was appreciated.[1]

Reference must be made to one other line of testimony. There were petitions presented to Congress from manufacturers and ship-builders praying for protection, and these are frequently referred to for the purpose of showing the existence of a protectionist sentiment. I do not pretend to have

---

[1] This Report was ordered to be reprinted in 1809. Other events in that year foreshadow the later development of protection.

examined all these petitions, but my impression is that, while they may indicate the presence of protectionist ideas in a slight degree, they by no means prove the prevalence of those ideas, nor that the question had ever been brought fairly before the public mind. The general fact is, that, about the year 1789, some considerable number of petitions were presented to Congress. But when, as will be explained hereafter, American shipping had secured the greater part of the world's carrying trade, the desire for manufactures seems to have passed away. When the treaty of Amiens gave peace to Europe in 1802, and European powers reclaimed their own commerce, petitions again made their appearance; but the interest which they evinced again disappeared when hostilities were renewed in the old world. There was, indeed, no decided movement toward manufactures till 1808, the year which marks the first downfall of American commerce. From this time on, one observes the ever-growing importance of petitions in the management of affairs in the United States, or, what amounts in principle to the same thing, the ever-growing importance of the "Third Branch of the Legislature." Government by petition is government by special interests, and for that reason one must be very careful in accepting requests for special legislation as evidence of public sentiment. Yet, giving all the weight that is claimed for petitions, it appears that they were not at all significant during the period we are studying, nor does Congress seem to have granted them much attention. Moreover, it should not be forgotten that they are to be interpreted in the same manner as the desire for independence of foreign, *i. e.*, English producers, and, in consequence, find their origin quite as much in political as in industrial considerations. A quotation from one of the petitions presented in 1789, will most clearly portray this phase of interpretation. It is as follows: "Your petitioners were early led to fear . . . . that their country, having gained the form of liberty, had left in the hands of their enemies the instrument of oppression and the spirit to exercise it. They soon perceived that their prospects of improving wealth were blasted by a system of commercial usurpation, originating in prejudice and fostered by a feeble government."[1]

The conclusion, then, to which this perhaps too extended discussion leads is, that the idea of protection in the United States was not in its origin a distinctly formulated industrial conception, but rather a subordinate part of a more extensive and decidedly aggressive political purpose; that, in the working out of this political purpose, especially after 1807, there were introduced conditions decidedly propitious to the growth of a protective policy as such; and that, in 1816, it stood forth no longer a subordinate part of a general policy, but itself an independent policy, making claims that would have startled the earlier statesmen. For an historical student, this may be pertinently presented by imagining the John Adams of 1783, and the John Quincy Adams of 1824 or 1828, indulging in a family chat on free trade and protection. The father would hardly have understood what the son meant.

The theory of interpretation here maintained can alone give continuity of development to the first twenty-five years of American history. Ideas such as are found in the American system of protection could not have sprung up in a day. The evidence is strong that, in 1783, fair treatment on the part of England would have secured freedom of commerce from the United States. But few of the States had expressed anything akin to protective tariffs in their laws, and, to suppose that, in 1789, the policy of trade restrictions stood forth as itself a master policy, is to assume an exception to all ordinary rules of historical development. For another such record of rapid development one must go beyond the limits of history and turn to those pages in Grecian mythology, describing the birth and growth of Hermes, the god of trade.

---

[1] American State Papers, Finance, Vol. I., p. 9.

In the morning an innocent babe, before the sun had reached the zenith, he had stolen and slaughtered the cattle of Apollo. It was from the commercial war of 1812 that the "American system" emerged, claiming for the first time in its own right the attention of the public. In 1794, Fisher Ames, a "protectionist," expressed surprise that manufacturers should like taxes rather than no taxes; and upon a motion to reduce the duties upon sugar said: "If the money was not likely to be wanted at all, it would be one good cause for dropping the taxes." Tench Coxe, writing the same year upon the American tariff, said: "It has been frequently observed in the course of the preceding pages, *that the duties laid for the purpose of revenue,* on foreign manufactures imported into the United States, are a great encouragement to similar articles, which are or shall be manufactured in this country."[1] In 1816, Clay declared for "a thorough and decided protection to home-manufactures by ample duties," and Mr. Ingham who supported him said: "The revenue was only an incidental consideration, and ought not to have any influence in the decision upon the proposition before the committee." The public sentiment which controlled the first Congress cannot be brought into harmony with that which controlled the fourteenth, or, indeed, with that which is potent with the Treasury Department to-day, and a true presentation of financial history must recognize this fact.

Including the tariff law of February 5, 1816, there were twenty acts of Congress during the first quarter of a century in our National history, relating to customs duties. It would be wearisome to speak in detail of all these acts, and in order to avoid such a necessity it has been my purpose to present in the following table, in a manner easily to be followed, the more important modifications of the tariff-system. Those articles only which are significant have been selected.

---

[1] View of the United States, p. 458.

	Iron of various kinds.	Steel, per cwt.	Cables, per cwt.	Linens.	Cottons.	Woolens.	Raw Cotton.	Glassware.	Carriages.	Salt, per bushel.	Gen'l *ad valorem* duties.	Teas, per pound. In American Ships from China.	Teas, per pound. In American Ships from Europe.	Teas, per pound. Otherwise imported.	Wines per gallon.	Spirits, per gallon. Distilled from grain.	Spirits, per gallon. Distilled from other material.
1789	7½	56	75	5	5	5[2]	free	10	15	10	5	6–20	8–26	15–45	10–18	8–10	
1790	...	75	100	...	7½	...	03[1]	12½	15½	12	...	10–32	12–40	15–50	20–35	12–25	
1791	...	...	...	...	...	...	...	...	...	...	...	....	....	....	.........[3]	20–40	
1792	10	100	180	7½	...	7½	...	15	...	...	7½	....	....	....	20–56	28–50	25–46
1794	15	...	...	12½	12½	10	...	...	20	...	10	....	....	....	....	....	....
1797	...	...	02[1]	...	15	...	...	...	...	20	...	12–32	14–40	17–50	....	....	....
1800	...	...	...	...	...	12½	...	...	...	...	12½	....	....	....	....	....	....
1804	17½	...	...	15	17½	15	...	17½	22½	...	15	....	....	....	28–58[3]	....	....
1812	35	200	04	30	35	30	06	35	45	free[4]	30	24–64	28–80	34–100	56–116	56–100	50–92

[1] Per pound.

[2] This is for unspecified woolens.

[3] Wines not specified charged 40 per cent. *ad valorem.*

[4] This article was made free in 1807, and charged again with 20 cts. per pound in 1813.

A glance at the foregoing table shows the constantly increasing rate of charges imposed by the government, beginning with the modest rate of five per cent. upon the general list, and rising to thirty per cent., yet every increase was in the presence of some demand that the administration regarded as pressing. The act of 1790 was to meet the financial necessities of the funding schemes. The law of 1792 was to raise money for the protection of the frontiers, and is especially interesting as embodying the Hamiltonian notion of protection. In his communication to Congress, Hamilton expressed the hope that in two years the exigency calling for increased revenue would pass away and that the rate upon the general list might be reduced, but, in 1794, not only was it found necessary to retain these duties, but to impose new. The law of 1797 was forced upon Congress by threatened foreign complications. "The French Revolution had just reached the highest point of settled delirium," and, though it was the desire of Mr. Adams and his cabinet to maintain strict neutrality, it was regarded as safe to expend something upon a navy. This law was really of more financial significance than appears from the table, for it not only imposed new duties, but made permanent those sections of the acts of 1792 and 1794 that terminated with 1797. The two and one-half per cent. increase of duties upon all imports (with ten per cent. additional if imported in other than American vessels) by the act of March 26, 1804, was to provide funds for the protection of commerce and seamen against the Barbary Powers, and formed what was called the "Mediterranean Fund." The act declared that this fund should cease three months after the conclusion of a treaty of peace with Tripoli. This event occurred in 1805, but the fund was continued by yearly acts till 1813, when it was made permanent, and so remained till March, 1815. The alleged temporary character of many of these laws, as notably the laws of 1792, 1794, and 1804, is perhaps the most singular fact in this period of our tariff-history, and the fact that no important duty once imposed, except that upon salt, was ever relinquished, shows with what ease and certainty a people may learn to bear taxes. No period in our history illustrates this more pertinently, unless it be the years after the outbreak of the Rebellion. The doubling of all duties in 1812 was expressly termed a war-tax, and was imposed for the purpose of securing means to carry on the struggle against England, a struggle that the war-party had at last succeeded in drawing upon the country. Whether or not it be in harmony with sound rules of finance to raise the rates of customs duties on the event of a commercial war, is a question that will be reserved for later consideration.

It is always regarded as significant information respecting the workings of a tariff-system, to learn the rates actually paid on goods imported. It is the purpose of the following table (p. 39) to present this information.

It is proper to say that these figures are estimates and therefore must be interpreted with some caution. The official returns for these years do not give the value of goods imported that are charged with specific duties, but the quantities only. For general purposes, however, the percentage-results may be relied upon, and the lesson which they seem to enforce is the unsteadiness in the actual rate of taxation previous to 1817, so far as the revenue system was based upon customs duties. One of the great delusions of American financiering is its over-estimation of the importance of tariff-laws. The secret of their approbation is simply that, in their workings, they are obscure.

It yet remains for us to consider briefly the technicalities of the tonnage-acts. In May, 1789, a resolution passed the House of Representatives to the effect that American-built vessels, owned by citizens of the United States, should pay, upon entering any port in the country, a duty of nine cents per ton; if of foreign build but owned by American citizens, six cents per ton; vessels belonging to subjects of foreign powers with which the United States had commercial treaties, thirty cents per ton; while vessels belonging to subjects of any other power should pay at the rate of fifty cents per ton. The Senate would not agree to this discrimination between foreign peoples, and the House was obliged, although

Year.	Value of Imports.	Imports for consumption.	Receipts from customs.	Percentage of customs on importation for consumption.	Percentage of customs on total imports.
1791	$ 29,200,000	$ 28,687,959	$ 4,399,473	15.34	15.07
1792	31,500,000	29,746,902	3,433,070	11.54	10.89
1793	31,100,000	28,990,428	4,255,306	14.68	13.68
1794	34,600,000	28,073,767	4,801,065	17.10	11.27
1795	69,756,268	61,266,796	5,588,461	11.21	8.01
1796	81,436,164	55,136,164	6,657,987	12.02	8.17
1797	75,379,406	48,379,406	7,549,649	15.60	10.02
1798	68,551,700	35,551,700	7,106,061	19.99	10.37
1799	79,069,148	33,446,148	6,610,449	19.70	8.31
1800	91,252,768	52,121,891	9,080,932	17.42	9.95
1801	111,363,511	64,720,790	10,750,778	16.61	9.66
1802	76,333,333	40,558,362	12,438,235	30.67	16.29
1803	64,666,666	51,072,594	10,479,417	20.52	16.21
1804	85,000,000	48,768,403	11,098,565	22.76	13.06
1805	120,600,000	67,420,981	12,936,487	19.19	10.73
1806	129,410,000	69,126,764	14,667,698	21.22	11.35
1807	138,500,000	78,856,442	15,845,521	20.09	11.49
1808	56,990,000	43,992,586	16,363,550	37.22	28.71
1809	59,400,000	38,602,469	7,257,506	18.80	12.22
1810	85,400,000	61,008,705	8,583,309	14.07	10.02
1811	53,400,000	37,377,210	13,313,222	35.62	24.93
1812	77,030,000	68,534,873	8,958,777	13.07	11.63
1813	22,005,000	19,157,135	13,224,623	69.03	60.09
1814	12,965,000	12,819,831	5,998,772	46.79	46.27
1815	113,041,274	106,457,924	7,282,942	6.84	6.44
1816	147,103,000	129,964,844	36,306,874	27.94	24.69

quite reluctantly, to abandon its purpose. This seems to have been a favorite policy with Madison, and at first looks like the strongest kind of protection, but the idea upon which it was based was rather that an unfriendly foreign power could be forced into friendly relations by discriminating commercial regulations. This was the reciprocity-policy in which Jefferson professed a belief, and it was the policy that gave form to the first phase of the "American System." The debates in regard to this whole question are very significant for the historian, since the opinion expressed in them forecast those two lines of foreign policy which controlled American politics for so many years. At present, however, we are precluded from entering upon a detailed analysis of them.

The tonnage act, as approved, made no distinction between the ships of foreign powers. It did, however, decidedly favor American shipping. The rate imposed upon American-built and American-owned ships was six cents per ton, while foreign-built and foreign-owned vessels were charged with thirty cents, and vessels both built and owned by foreign subjects were imposed with an entry-fee of fifty cents per ton. In this manner did the United States attempt to pay back England in her own coin and to maintain a share in the carrying trade.

The foreign relations, in view of which the first tonnage and tariff acts were passed, have already been presented; in order, however, to understand the workings of the system thus established, it will be necessary to go a little farther into the subject and notice some facts in European politics which materially affected not only the sources from which revenue arose, but also the further development of the system.

The period which thus comes under observation is one of public disorder. Europe was thrown into commotion in consequence of the French Revolution, and it was found impossible for even neutral states to escape the results of hostilities. In 1793, Great Britain, Spain, Prussia, and Germany entered into an alliance, which, in addition to prohibiting exportation of stores from their own ports to France, bound the contracting parties "to take all other measures in their power for injuring the commerce of France," and to unite their efforts "to prevent all other powers not implicated in this war, from giving, on this occasion of common concern to every civilized State, any protection whatever, directly or indirectly, in consequence of their neutrality, to the commerce and property of the French, on the sea or in the ports of France."[1] The United States was the only nation of importance not drawn into this controversy, and her policy, openly declared, was to maintain the strictest neutrality. On the 16th of December, 1793, Jefferson, who was then Secretary of State, submitted to Congress a report upon the Commercial relations which the United States sustained to the nations of the world. From this report it appears that the policy of the European States was to prohibit, either by edict or high duties, all American produce, when such produce, even at greater cost to themselves, might be derived from their own colonies. Thus European States hoped to retain the trade of their own possessions. To meet these restrictions Jefferson knew of but two methods: friendly relations, or counter-legislation. He much preferred the former. "Would even a single nation," said he, "begin with the United States this system of free commerce, it would be advisable to begin it with that nation." But since no nation was willing to enter upon such relations it was his advice to Congress to adopt measures founded in reciprocity, "to return to each nation exactly what the United States received from it."[2] Upon the basis of this report, Madison based those resolutions which revived the rejected policy of 1789, but this time, in addition to discriminating tonnage duties favoring nations in alliance with the United States, he proposed special duties on leather, metals, cotton, woolens and silk, the products of nations not joined to this country by treaty; and, with reference to the West India trade, he desired additional duties on all importations by foreign vessels from ports to which American vessels were not admitted. This time, however, he could not carry the House with him. In

---

[1] The proportion of carrying trade done by American ships for England and France respectively, was $3\frac{1}{10}$ to 1.

[2] American State Papers, Vol. I., p. 300.

1794, John Jay was sent to England for the purpose of negotiating a treaty which should secure to this country those rights to which she was entitled on the high seas, but which, by the treaty of the Allied powers, were, to say the least, endangered. It was certainly an opportune time for the negotiation of a treaty. British commerce was for the time rendered uncertain, and British colonies were beginning to suffer from the want of the means of safe exchange. The following table will present clearly the relative effect upon England and America of this period of endangered commerce.

Year.	American tonnage employed in foreign trade.	British tonnage employed in American trade.
1789	127,329	94,110
1792	414,679	206,065
1794	525,649	37,058
1796	675,046	19,669

The treaty which Jay succeeded in negotiating allowed reciprocal trade between British Dominions in Europe and the United States; but the twelfth article prohibited the exportation to Europe of commodities which were products of the West Indies, and confined the trade of the United States with British colonies to the extent of our own consumption. This article, however, was rejected by Congress, so that the West India trade was continued under former conditions; that is, it was subject to the regulations of the British orders in council and was based upon sufferance rather than stipulated right.[1]

In order that the treaty of the Allied powers might be enforced, there was issued, from the Council of Great Britain,

[1] Causes and consequences of Orders in Council, by Alexander Baring, p. 24.

an order instructing cruisers "to stop and detain for lawful adjudication all ships laden with goods which were the produce of any French colony, or carrying provisions, or other supplies, for the use of any such colony."[1] The rigor of this was afterward somewhat abated, until by an order of January, 1798, freedom of trade was permitted to neutrals with the colonies of enemies. This order was termed an indulgence and remained in force until the treaty of Amiens.

The French policy in view of the treaty of the Allied powers is found formally expressed in a decree of 1796, which declared that "the French will treat neutral nations in the manner they suffer themselves to be treated by the English." In 1790, American vessels were obliged to take out a "rôle d'équipage" under penalty of being declared "good prizes." In 1798, contrary to the stipulation of the treaty, which declared that free ships should make free goods, a decree was issued, providing that the character of vessels should be determined by that of their cargoes, and that any ship having on board merchandise coming from British possessions should be considered a "good prize," whoever might be the owner of the merchandise. On the assumption that France was in earnest in issuing these decrees, had she possessed a navy adequate to their vigorous enforcement, American shipping must have been swept from the seas; but it is more than likely that these decrees were issued with a view to their effect on American politics, and it is certain that they did not injuriously influence the American carrying trade, which at this time had become considerable.

The answer which the American Congress made to these encroachments was to grant merchant vessels the right of defending themselves from search or seizure, to proclaim void the French treaty of 1778, and to declare as a lawful prize any armed vessel sailing under the French flag.

---

[1] One may find all the important Orders in Council, and French Decrees in Seybert's Statistics.

During this period, America, as the only important neutral power, had enjoyed the carrying trade of Europe. While the temporary peace of Amiens lasted, her commerce was restricted to the carrying of her own produce; but, upon the renewal of hostilities, her neutrality again secured to her the lucrative West India trade. This state of affairs continued till the year 1807, when the commercial relations of America to Europe were radically changed. In the first place, the Jay treaty expired and the privileges of direct trade were lost. But the closing in of the two great combatants for the final struggle brought to this country yet greater consequences. Napoleon well knew that the source of England's vitality was her commerce and trade, and that if he could destroy this, his supremacy in Europe was an accomplished fact. This was the purpose of his Berlin decree which appeared November 21, 1806. This decree closed all European ports to Great Britain and threatened the seizure of American vessels trading in British goods. The rejoinder on the part of England was to subject all vessels to search, and any bound to those ports from which the British flag was excluded were liable to compulsory detention in England. Then followed the Milan decree of 1807, which declared that any vessel submitting to such search should be considered "denationalized." These measures did not, as in the former case, mean a paper warfare, but they meant rather the annihilation of all neutral rights. It was their purpose to force the United States to take one side or the other in this controversy. The French party was at this time in the ascendency, and the regulations of the United States were aimed at England rather than France. In 1807, Congress laid an embargo on all American shipping by means of which it was thought to make England sensible of the dependence of her manufactories upon this country for raw material. Though severely felt in England, as shown by petitions to Parliament to which the embargo gave rise, the English government refused to alter its policy; but such was the opposition to the embargo in the United States that, after being subjected to modifications, so as at one time to be a non-exportation act, and at another a non-communication act with England or France, it was wholly abandoned. This occurred in June, 1809. The war of 1812 with its necessary commercial restrictions closes this chapter of commercial orders, decrees, and regulations, the importance of which cannot be overestimated in searching for the true interpretation of this first period of tonnage and tariff-acts. A consideration of the effects of these diplomatic events upon the financial and industrial development of the country, will be reserved till the last chapter of this essay.

II.—INTERNAL DUTIES AND DIRECT TAXES.

Internal Duties.

The first form of internal duties laid in the United States was an excise duty upon distilled spirits. The first law for this purpose was approved March 3, 1791, which, however, gave place to the permanent law of May 8, 1792. These bills were not passed without opposition. Those who opposed them urged that they contemplated a tax which was unpopular, and which would be unprofitable because unpopular; that an excise tax of any kind was dangerous to the liberties of the people and would, on that account, meet with especial opposition in the Southern States. Some members expressed themselves as favoring a poll-tax, although, if Mr. Madison's opinions be accepted, the sentiment of neither the House nor the country would admit of a direct tax of any kind. In favor of the bill it was urged that tariff duties had been extended as far as the interests of trade would allow, and that an increase of revenue was essential; also, that the proposed tax would tend to discourage the consumption of spirits, which was very great and hurtful to the health, morals, and economy of the community; and that, in the form in which it was proposed, it would act as an encouragement to agriculture. The second bill passed the House by a vote of 35 to 21, yet many voted for it who had expressed themselves against the principle of an excise tax, and had it been attempted at that time to extend this form of securing a revenue to any article but spirits, it is doubtful if such an attempt could have succeeded.

By the law of 1792, all spirits distilled within the United States were imposed with an excise duty as follows.

Spirits Distilled

From foreign materials.				*From material produced in the U. S.*			
First class of proof,		10 cts.	per gal.	First class of proof,		7 cts.	per gal.
Second "	"	11	"	Second "	"	8	"
Third "	"	12	"	Third "	"	9	"
Fourth "	"	14	"	Fourth "	"	11	"
Fifth "	"	18	"	Fifth "	"	13	"
Sixth "	"	25	"	Sixth "	"	18	"

This expression foreign material, as here used, means West India molasses and sugar, as distinguished from barley and corn of domestic growth. From the former was manufactured New England rum, which was conceived to be the most pernicious article of drink known. In addition to this discrimination in favor of whiskies and against rums, it will be remembered that molasses, as a raw material, was already subject to an impost duty. To diminish the manufacture of these pernicious rums by substituting for them spirits distilled from materials which were the growth of home soil, and at the same time to increase the demand for home agricultural products, was the avowed purpose of this discrimination favoring whiskies. For small stills it was made optional with the owner to pay ten cents per month per gallon on the capacity of the still, or seven cents per gallon on the amount of spirits, actually distilled.

Opposition to this form of taxation extended beyond the doors of Congress. In Pennsylvania, North Carolina, Virginia, and Maryland, there were resolutions passed denouncing the measure; and, as will be remembered, in Pennsylvania the execution of the law gave rise to that chapter in the history of the United States commonly called "The Whiskey Insurrection." It will be impossible to insert here even a brief sketch of this movement, but a presentation of the ideas of the insurgents and of the interests which they conceived to be endangered, may be allowed as pertinent. Under the colonial government of Pennsylvania, there had been two attempts to impose a tax upon spirits, one in 1756, and the other in 1772; but neither had met with any success in the Western counties.[1] A similar effort also on the part of the government of New Jersey had not proved successful, a fact well known in Pennsylvania, while in other neighboring States there had been no excise law. The intelligent opposition to this Federal tax may be found stated in the minutes of the Pittsburg meeting of August 22, 1792.[2] The clerk of this meeting, it may be interesting to remark, was Albert Gallatin, who afterwards came to be the directing member of the Jefferson cabinet. It was urged at this meeting that a tax upon spirits operated in proportion to numbers rather than wealth, and in consequence was unjust in itself and oppressive to the poor; and in addition to this, that all taxes upon articles of consumption, because of the power that must necessarily be vested in the officers who collect them, will in the end destroy the liberty of any people that permits them to be introduced. The course of reasoning here presented is the same as that urged in Congress against a tax on salt, when it was maintained that such a tax was in reality a poll-tax, and as such did not meet the requirements of equality as measured by the amount of property controlled. The condition of the western counties of Pennsylvania was something of an excuse for the conduct of their inhabitants. Whiskey was so common and money

[1] Findley's History of the Insurrection, ch. II.

[2] Pennsylvania Archives, 2nd Series, Vol. IV., p. 30.

was so scarce that the former served as a medium of exchange in trade, yet would not be accepted in payment of the tax, which, computed in money, amounted to fully one-third of the price of the article.[1] The attorney-general, so it is stated, could find no basis for legal proceedings against the insurgents, and it was not until militia had been put on foot by order of the President, that the people were induced to submit. In other quarters of the Union where the execution of the law was opposed, the proclamation of the President sufficed to restore order and secure acquiescence. This, it will be observed, was the first form which opposition to internal duties assumed in the United States.

The second object attached by the system of internal taxation was carriages used "for the conveyance of persons." The permanent law for this purpose, which repealed a law of two years previous, was approved May 28, 1796. These two enactments did not differ as to the mode of apportionment, but the rate of duty was raised by the latter act so that the law, as approved, stood as follows:

Coaches driven by box or postilion	$15 per year.
Chariots	12 " "
Coaches with panels	9 " "
Coaches without panels	6 " "
Two-wheeled top carriages	3 " "
Other two-wheeled carriages	2 " "

Nothing in this act was to be construed so as to levy any tax upon wagons used in agriculture or for the transportation of commodities.

The execution of this law did not, as in the case of the excise on spirits, meet with open opposition; nevertheless the idea of visible taxes had not become so familiar that their collection was permitted without expressions of disapprobation. In the present instance, the constitutionality of the law

[1] Findley's History of the Insurrection, p. 41.

was attacked in the well known case of Hylton vs. the United States. The ground of argument was simple and the decision direct. The question upon which the case turned was, whether a tax levied under the above mentioned law was direct or indirect within the meaning of the Constitution; if indirect, it was admitted to be rightly laid; but if direct, the point was urged that it was unconstitutional because not laid by the rule of apportionment prescribed in the Constitution. The Supreme Court decided that the duty upon carriages was not a direct tax, and the reasons submitted in support of this decision were the following: that the Constitution contemplated no tax as direct except capitation and land taxes; that a tax laid upon carriages by apportionment among the several States would be unequal and unjust, since the number of carriages was entirely out of proportion to the federal population in the various parts of the country; also, that indirect taxes include all taxes imposed upon expenses or consumption, and that "a carriage for the conveyance of persons" is a consumable commodity.[1]

From this time opposition to internal duties was confined to political measures. The fact that the Federalists had imposed them and had insisted that the laws should be executed served as a powerful argument in the hands of their enemies during the campaign of 1800.

In 1794, the system of internal taxation was extended so as to include three new sources of revenue. A tax was levied upon the sale of certain liquors, an excise duty was imposed upon the manufacture of snuff and the refining of sugar, and the proceeds of auction-sales were also laid under contribution. The first of these required retailers of wines and foreign spirits to pay a yearly license of five dollars. Snuff was made to bear eight cents, and sugar two cents per pound, when prepared in the United States. The revenue which proceeded from the snuff-tax did not warrant its con-

---

[1] 3 Dall., 171.

tinuance: it was first changed to a tax upon snuff-mills, which tax, in its turn, was suspended by yearly acts until, in 1800, the duty was abolished.

The tax upon auction-sales was at the rate of twenty-five cents upon every one hundred dollars which were proceeds from the sale of goods connected with husbandry, and fifty cents upon like amounts arising from sale of any other sort of goods. Three years later still another source of internal revenue was opened by the approval of an act levying duties upon certain legal transactions. Stamps were used as the means of collecting this duty, the rates imposed being as follows:

Certificate of admission to practice in any United States Court	$10 00
Certificate of Naturalization	5 00
Any grant under seal of the United States	4 00
Any certified copy of such grant	2 00
Certified bonds, etc.	1 00
Any paper requiring the seal of a Court	50
Any instrument connected with the execution of a will	According to value of instrument.
Any insurance policy	According to value of instrument.
All bonds and notes	According to value of instrument.

The list of internal duties imposed previous to 1813, and properly falling under the classification of indirect taxes, has now been presented. For the administration of this system, the several States were accepted as revenue districts, each district being divided at the discretion of the President into surveys of inspection. For each district there was a supervisor, and for each survey as many inspectors as the supervisor deemed necessary.

Direct Taxes.

Notwithstanding increase in the rate of custom dues and the establishment of a system of indirect taxes, the annual income was not adequate to the needs of the government, and, in the judgment of the administration, it appeared desirable to open yet another source of revenue. The most potent consideration, however, in resorting to direct taxation was found in the threatening attitude of foreign affairs and in the fact that a commercial war would greatly diminish the revenue from customs.

As early as 1794 the special committee on public credit recommended a direct tax of $750,000. In the same report there was also a recommendation in favor of stamp duties; both were at the time rejected, but two years later "the existing and approaching exigencies" appeared so pressing that both measures again found strong recommendation. Mr. Wolcott was at this time Secretary of the Treasury, and a request from Congress for a plan to raise $2,000,000 by direct taxation gave rise to his most important state paper. The problem which the Secretary undertook to solve was by no means a light one. His task consisted in drafting a law which would meet the constitutional requirements of a direct tax and yet be sufficiently elastic to adjust itself to the various customs in the separate States. He first instituted an inquiry respecting the several methods of State-taxation, and the information secured showed that there existed the greatest diversity, both as regards subjects selected for the imposition of taxes, and also respecting methods of apportionment and collection. It would be a weary undertaking to follow minutely this voluminous report, and it has been my purpose to render such a task unnecessary by preparing a tabular statement of its most interesting and pertinent facts.

When one learns that the report from which the following table is drawn covers fifty pages in a quarto volume, he need not be reminded that its salient features only are here presented. For more particular information respecting early local taxation the student is referred to the report itself, which will be found in the first volume of American State Papers relating to the subject of finance. As a study in local administration it contains an abundance of interesting matter. Thus in the

States.	Uniform capitation tax.	Tax on horses and cattle.	All farm stock valued.[3]	Taxes imposed on mass of property.[4]	Mode of taxing lands.	Collectors appointed.				
						By People.	By Legislature.	By State Executive.	By Court.	By County Officers.
Vermont	×	×	...	...	According to quantity, if enclosed	×	...	...	...	...
New Hampshire	×	×	...	...	According to annual rent	×	...	...	...	...
Massachusetts	×	×	...	...	According to annual rent	×	...	...	...	...
Connecticut	×	×	...	...	Included in mass of property	×	...	...	...	...
Rhode Island	×	...	×	×	According to state of cultivation	×	...	...	...	...
New York	...	...	×	×	Included in mass of property	×	...	...	...	...
New Jersey	...	×	...	...	*Ad valorem*, according to value in different countries	×	...	...	...	...
Pennsylvania	...	×	...	...	*Ad valorem*, according to triennial assessment	×	...	...	...	...
Delaware	...	...	×	×	Included in mass of property	...	...	...	...	×
Maryland	...[1]	...	×	×	*Ad valorem*, upon valuation in different countries	...	...	...	...	×
Virginia	...	×[2]	...	...	According to permanent valuation	...	...	×[5]	...	...
Kentucky	...	×	...	...	Uniformly by quality, all lands divided into three classes	×[5]	...	...	...	...
North Carolina	×	...	...	...	Uniformly by quantity	...	...	...	×[5]	...
South Carolina	...	...	...	...	Uniformly by districts	...	×	...	...	...
Georgia	×	...	...	...	Uniformly by districts	...	×	...	...	...

[1] A poll tax is contrary to the Constitution of Maryland. For a history of the poll tax in Maryland, see an interesting article by L. W. Wilhelm in the *Magazine of American History*, for *January*, 1884.

[2] Cattle excepted.

[3] In other States all farm stock and implements were exempt.

[4] Other States designate special objects.

[5] The sheriff appointed if able to qualify.

harmony of custom respecting taxation within certain restricted sections, there is disclosed the common origin and previous history of certain of the colonies, and there is suggested some intimacy of intercourse between them. For example, the revenue systems of the New England section conform quite well to the same general model. Some of the Southern States, also, present many features in common. As between these sections, however, and indeed as between the States also, the more one studies the details of the systems, the greater differentiation does he observe, a fact which goes to show how isolated and local these sections must have been before they were united by the common bond of complaint. Thus the lists of exemptions varied materially in the several States; the position occupied by the negro before the revenue laws was not the same in all localities; so far as capital employed in business or money loaned at interest was taxed, one can discover no harmony whatever in principles of attachment; discretion granted assessors, also, presents the widest variety of custom. One of the curious points of contrast, and one that brings strongly into contrast the respective characters of the people at this early time, pertains to the custom of perfecting the taxable lists among the Northern and the Southern peoples. In Connecticut, the inhabitants were classed according to the religious societies to which they belonged, the church thus serving as the centre from which the work of the assessor started; in North Carolina and Georgia, on the other hand, it was usual for the captains of the militia to advertise a muster to which the people repaired with lists of their property. Thus, in the one case, the church-rolls, and in the other the rolls of the militia captains, were accepted as the most complete enumeration of taxable inhabitants.

Since, however, this essay pertains to Federal rather than local taxation, we are precluded from following farther the facts presented in this report. Its only importance for our present purpose is to show upon what ground Secretary Wolcott based his decision in favor of a Federal revenue system independent of local customs. So clearly did he recognize the conflicting character of the local revenue systems, that he conceived it impossible to make use of State-machinery for National taxation, and advocated the establishment of a new and independent system receiving its authority altogether from the central government.

Some of the ideas respecting this system as they lay in his mind, may not be uninteresting. A capitation tax was rejected because it had a tendency to raise wages and thus discourage manufactures; it threw an undue portion of the burden of the public expense on the middle class of farmers; and, so strong was the opposition to it in various parts of the Union, that it was believed the expense of collecting it would be out of proportion to the net revenue arising from it.

A tax on farm produce was opposed because unequal. Taxes on capital were not considered advisable because, if the incidence rested with the capitalist, money would be driven from the country, while if it were possible for the tax to be incorporated with the price of any commodity, it would cease to be direct. Taxes on profits arising from certain employments were considered arbitrary and unequal, although they were favored by the ease with which they might be collected. A tax upon land was regarded from some points of view as good, since it would be uniform, certain, and equal.

In May, 1798, Wolcott submitted another report which contained his plan for a direct tax. It was to be addressed to individuals and to attach the following articles: (*a*) on dwelling houses, to be distributed into nine classes and taxed uniformly in each class; (*b*) on slaves, to be taxed uniformly, 50 cents per caput; (*c*) on lands, to be taxed *ad valorem* in each State at such rate as with the other taxes would produce the sum apportioned. The interesting part of this plan, so far as the method of apportionment is concerned, appears in connection with the house tax. The classes into which Mr. Wolcott divided dwellings and the rates which he proposed were:

First	class,	of value	from $	80 to	$ 200,	to bear	a tax	of $	.50
Second	"	"	"	200 to	600,	"	"	"	1.50
Third	"	"	"	600 to	1,200,	"	"	"	3.00
Fourth	"	"	"	1,200 to	2,000,	"	"	"	6.00
Fifth	"	"	"	2,000 to	4,000,	"	"	"	12.00
Sixth	"	"	"	4,000 to	6,000,	"	"	"	20.00
Seventh	"	"	"	6,000 to	10,000,	"	"	"	30.00
Eighth	"	"	"	10,000 to	25,000,	"	"	"	60.00
Ninth	"	"	"	25,000 and	upwards,	"	"	"	120.00

The influence which Hamilton had upon Wolcott is well known, yet this plan of a house tax was not Hamilton's, nor did it meet his approval. The one which he suggested, through Mr. Sedgwick and Mr. Smith, was entirely different, being based upon the principle of rating houses according to the number of rooms they contained. According to his plan

A log house				was to bear	a tax	of $	.20.	
A house	of	two	rooms	"	"	"	.25	per room.
"	"	three	"	"	"	"	.33⅓	"
"	"	four	"	"	"	"	.40	"
"	"	five	"	"	"	"	.60	"
"	"	six	"	"	"	"	.75	"
"	"	seven	" and upward	"	"	"	1.00	"

The law which finally passed in 1798 did not incorporate the ideas of either Hamilton or Wolcott, but conformed to a plan traceable to the advice of Albert Gallatin. This law provided for a progressive percentage tax upon houses classified according to value.

Houses valued from		$100 to $1,000	were taxed upon the dollar at the rate of		.002
"	"	1,000 to 3,000	"	"	.004
"	"	3,000 to 6,000	"	"	.005
"	"	6,000 to 10,000	"	"	.006
"	"	10,000 to 15,000	"	"	.007
"	"	15,000 to 20,000	"	"	.008
"	"	20,000 to 30,000	"	"	.009
"	"	30,000 and upward	"	"	.01

The rejection of the Wolcott plan must meet with approbation. It was based on no principle of economy and was neither equal nor just. In its workings it would have contradicted the rule which Congress professed to have accepted as the basis of its impositions. The percentage of taxation on different houses in the same class was not uniform, although the rate of taxation was; and such discrimination as existed lay against the poorer house. This may be easily perceived by comparing the percentage rate of taxation on different classes and the different rates in the same class.

	Highest rate, viz: on poorest house.	Lowest rate, viz: on best house.
First class,	.006$\frac{1}{4}$	.002$\frac{1}{2}$
Second class,	.007$\frac{1}{2}$	.002$\frac{1}{2}$
Eighth class,	.006	.002$\frac{2}{5}$
Ninth class,	.004$\frac{4}{5}$	Rate decreases as value increases.

Or taking the two extreme cases which the schedule renders possible, a house which is worth $200 would be imposed with a rate of .0075 on valuation, while a house assessed at $599 would be called upon to pay at the rate of only .0026; or, by comparing the highest rate in the second class with the lowest rate in the eighth, it appears that the poorer house pays the rate of .00425 higher than a house worth four times its value.

Hamilton's plan, which is apparently so arbitrary, is based upon the idea that rental may be regarded as the true criterion of what real estate should pay, and he claimed in its support that, by practical application to houses in his own vicinity, the ratio between the rate and rent was sufficiently accurate to meet the demands of justice. It must also be admitted that his method of assessment would obviate expense and uncertainty of valuation. On the other hand it might have a tendency to act in some cases as did the old English window- and hearth-tax, and result in the building of houses inferior to those that otherwise would be erected.

The plan adopted gave rise to a law that was French in its character, based on the principle of "l'impôt progressif," which was then playing, and has since played, so conspicuous a rôle in theories for the reorganization of society. Five years before, the French Assembly had adopted this mode of taxation, and the American house-tax of 1798 was an application of the same idea, although so drawn as to exhibit the most objectionable features of this method of impost. There was too great a discrepancy between the burdens imposed on different grades of property. Since this law is traceable to Gallatin, and since Gallatin was himself of French extraction and education, it is natural for one to search for some connection between the principle of taxation adopted by the Republicans of France and this law. But there appears to be no evidence of such connection, and a close study of the character of Gallatin does not permit one to regard him as an ardent admirer of all that is French. The collection of this direct tax was placed in the hands of those who already had charge of the execution of the internal revenue laws, the supervisors having full power to appoint additional collectors if they deemed it necessary.

In 1801, upon the accession of Jefferson to the Presidency, it was endeavored to change radically the financial policy of the United States. Of the six causes which the historian Hildreth mentions as resulting in the downfall of the Federal party, two are financial. The first was the six per cent. loan; the second, the direct tax. With regard to the latter, Hamilton said in a speech delivered before the electors of the State of New York, which was intended to influence their votes in favor of the Federal party, that it had ever been the policy of himself and associates to refrain from a resort to direct taxation except in the presence of threatened or actual hostilities, thus showing that the leaders of this party thought it expedient to apologize for having imposed a direct tax.

The new administration lost no time in redeeming its pledge, and, in 1802, all internal and direct taxes were abolished, not to be again reimposed until the commercial war of 1812 had endangered the revenue which flowed from the customs duties. The Jay treaty expired in 1807, and from that time the war-party gained rapidly in strength. In his financial reports of 1807 and 1808, Gallatin submitted statements which led Congress to the belief that war might be carried on without a resort to either direct or indirect taxation. The advocates of the war made efficient use of these reports. The financial measures which the Secretary had proposed were not adopted, and in 1812 the public treasury was not in a condition to sustain a war, and it was found necessary, in addition to doubling the customs rates, to establish again a system of internal revenue. These taxes were expressly termed war-taxes, the words being printed in italics, and the purpose of entailing upon the people a permanent and ever progressing system of taxation was explicitly disavowed. It thus appears that the people of the United States had not outgrown their fear of visible taxes, and still preferred to pay the legitimate expenses of the government with blindfolded eyes. Nor can one refrain from the observation in passing, that the financial disasters and absurd treasury-management which the history of this conflict discloses, finds its origin in the law that destroyed the system of internal revenue so laboriously established by the Federalists. The embarrassments occasioned by the absence of any machinery by which wealth currently created could be reached, teaches the lesson that a wise financial policy will provide in time of peace for the exigencies of increased expenditure during time of war. This was the defense presented by Wolcott for the maintenance of his expensive system of internal duties. "In case of foreign war," he said, "the revenue from customs will be greatly decreased, it is wise to provide some means of making up the deficiency." It is, indeed, a question worthy of serious consideration whether any people can afford to be without a system of duties that keeps at least in working order the machinery for levying duties directly upon current products.

So far as the form of indirect duties is concerned, this second period of their use presents very little change from the plan previously adopted; for direct taxes, however, Mr.

Gallatin established a system much more simple than the one incorporated in the law of 1798. The law of 1813 provided for a general assessment upon all taxable property according to its money-value. The apportionment of the tax among the several States was of course controlled by the conditions of the Constitution, but the apportionment of the State-tax to the counties in the State, which was accomplished through a direct act of Congress, was according to the assessed value of property in each county. The position of Mr. Gallatin in reference to direct taxes may be gathered from the following quotation: "Direct taxes are liable to peculiar objection, arising from the unavoidable inequality produced by the general rule of the Constitution. Whatever difference may exist between the relative wealth and consequent ability of paying of the several States, still the tax must necessarily be raised in proportion to their relative population. Should it, however, become necessary to resort to that resource, it is believed that a tax raised upon that species of property in each State which by the State laws is liable to State taxation, as had originally been contemplated by Congress, would be preferable to a general assessment, laid uniformly on the same species of property in all the States, as was ultimately adopted."[1]

In order also to placate the State authorities, and veil so far as possible the central authority that stood behind this tax, it was further provided that any State legislature might revise the Congressional apportionment of the tax among the counties, if the governmental distribution of burden was conceived to be unjust; and, in addition to this, each State was permitted to pay the apportioned amount directly out of its public treasury, in which case a deduction of fifteen per cent. was allowed. This was bringing into use again the theory of requisitions which had proved so disastrous under the Confederacy, but with this essential difference: there now existed the authority to coerce payment and the means to enforce it.

---

[1] See Report for 1807.

The machinery for collecting internal revenue was subjected to some slight modification. The States were divided into a number of collection-districts, with a principal assessor and collector for each, "who should be a respectable free-holder and reside in the district." The office of supervisor was abolished and the number of assistant assessors could at any time be reduced by the Secretary of the Treasury. The difference between the Gallatin and the Wolcott plan seems to have been that the former incorporated so far as possible the existing systems of the several States, and was so drawn as to avoid provoking popular hostility by ignoring local sentiment: while the latter introduced a new and uniform method of taxation which, to say the least, was strange in many parts of the Union and opposed in many instances to the habits of the people. Something respecting the financial consequence of these two systems will be presented in the study that follows.

III.—CRITICISMS UPON REVENUE LEGISLATION.

Having traced the development of the first period of taxation in the United States, and discovered as nearly as possible the conditions of this country at the time when the revenue system took its rise, it lies next in our purpose to consider the practical workings of the system during the period that it was in operation, and to answer such historical queries as may present themselves. It is to this task that our attention is at present turned.

It will be remembered that the chief object of the act of 1789 was to strengthen the public credit,[1] and, consequently, the question that naturally claims first attention concerns the influence exerted by the law upon the price of public securities. The resources of the country were ample to meet all

[1] Compare foot-note, Benton's Debates, Vol. I., p. 84.

obligations and the knowledge of this fact was widely spread; but, in order to raise the credit of the country, it was also necessary that Congress should express in law its willingness to provide for all debts and to create through law the machinery requisite to render the national resources available. It was necessary, as stated by Mr. Madison, "to revive those principles of honor and honesty that have too long lain dormant;" but, this being done by the rational method of opening a source of permanent revenue, the credit of the country was sure to revive. The facts show that this expectation was not in the least delusive. Before the date at which the law practically went into effect—the 15th of November—public securities had risen thirty-three and one-third per cent. higher than they were at the beginning of the year, and, by January 14, 1790, they had experienced an additional rise of fifty per cent. In the second message to Congress presented by Washington, the country was congratulated on "its rising credit and respectability." It may, however, be interesting to notice that this growth in financial respectability was due to the passing of the law, rather than to the actual revenue accruing on account of the law; for the fact is, that revenue arising from customs did not for a number of years suffice for both the payment of current interest upon the public debt and the contingent expenses of the government. During the first seven years of our National existence, receipts from loans, treasury notes, etc., amounted to some twenty millions of dollars, an insignificant sum as it now appears, but yet equal to two and a half times the average annual receipts of the government for the first eight years of reported returns. It was not until 1799 that the revenue from customs equalled the sum which, in 1789, was demanded by the estimates for public needs. This deficiency of income from customs was, however, the result of policy rather than of poverty. The first important State paper, pertaining to financial affairs, gave expression to the opinion that "to make provision equal to the funding of the whole debt would require the extension of taxation to a degree and to objects which the true interest of the public creditors forbids."

The other sources of revenue open to the government, apart from external and internal taxation, were the following: sale of public lands, sale of bank stock or dividends upon such shares as were retained, loans and treasury notes, the postage-department, and miscellaneous sources,—including forfeits, fines and the like; yet, from the beginning of the government until 1816, revenue arising from customs duties constituted more than six-elevenths of that arising from all other sources combined.

One cannot insist too strongly upon the political importance of these revenue laws, nor assign too great solicitude to the friends of the new government while the revenue system was under discussion. The early American statesmen recognized clearly the lever that was to set their hardly-wrought State in motion. The establishment of revenue and credit was the practical step which ensured the realization of that for which they so long had toiled, and it was this purpose, and not to establish the manufacture of beer bottles or encourage the growth of hemp, that was continually before their minds. He who does not recognize this is not in mental harmony with the period, and so fails to grasp the true meaning of these first debates. The safety of the Republic at that time was bound up with its ability and willingness to pay its honest debts. Legal provision for this was secured, and government became a reality. It was also through the influence which public honesty exerted upon private confidence that the country was launched upon its first period of commercial and industrial prosperity.

Recognizing, then, the early revenue system as adequate to the political and industrial necessities of the period, the next question that naturally presents itself is concerning the efficiency of revenue administration. The mark of a well-administered system of taxation is economy in collection, for this means not only a well-organized force, but also that the financial policy of the government harmonizes with the wishes of the public. It will be necessary in this connection to consider three forms of revenue: customs duties, internal duties, and direct taxes.

The expensiveness of customs dues, for the period previous to 1816, may be learned from the following table, which presents both gross and net revenue from customs, the cost of collection, and the percentage-cost estimated upon gross revenue after deducting drawbacks upon goods exported. The discrepancies observed between the gross amount received and the sum of the net amount and cost of collection, is explained by the fact that payments on drawbacks have been omitted from the table:

	Gross am't revenue from customs.	Net amount of revenue.	Expense of collection.	Cost per ct. collection.
1791	$ 6,873,783	$ 6,534,263	$240,031	.035
1792	5,095,919	4,614,924	161,932	.034
1793	6,720,985	6,073,512	188,915	.03
1794	8,671,195	6,683,318	222,128	.032
1795	11,253,733	7,959,409	260,845	.031
1796	12,681,867	7,368,970	292,478	.039
1797	13,001,105	8,258,111	345,757	.041
1798	11,528,091	6,193,280	376,063	.057
1799	15,439,569	9,037,437	412,798	.043
1800	16,181,425	9,353,362	444,313	.045
1801	20,828,240	13,362,702	482,899	.035
1802	15,150,428	8,327,335	492,905	.056
1803	14,523,652	11,322,551	406,814	.034
1804	20,799,635	14,977,085	495,084	.032
1805	23,897,664	14,980,218	558,688	.036
1806	26,538,987	16,081,976	614,548	.036
1807	27,323,227	16,493,434	646,110	.037
1808	11,348,694	7,181,714	568,292	.072
1809	11,843,576	7,139,037	503,905	.066
1810	16,898,539	12,757,988	447,868	.034
1811	10,660,666	7,872,528	443,936	.053
1812	15,300,910	13,040,121	481,745	.035
1813	7,965,568	6,533,603	417,939	.06
1814	4,806,022	4,381,882	359,169	.075
1815	38,990,036	37,656,486	510,557	.013
1816	33,558,960	28,572,281	820,423	.028

It thus appears that, for the first twenty-five years of our National life, the average cost of collecting customs duties was something less than four per cent. of gross receipts. The table further shows that this cost fluctuated with the state of commerce, and thus was largely independent of the control of Congress or the Treasury Department, a fact which, when well understood, presents a severe criticism upon this method of raising revenue. At present, the average cost of collecting customs duties is about three per cent. During the period corresponding to the one covered by this essay, the cost of collecting the English revenue was about five per cent.,[1] although reaching at times as high as seven; and, in France, under the administration of Neckar, the transfer of taxes from the pockets of citizens to the public chest consumed ten per cent. of the gross payment.[2] There is, however, an element of error in this latter comparison, for customs payments on the one side have been compared with total revenue on the other; still, as such a large proportion of revenue in the United States arose out of import duties, the error here noticed is probably less than would have been introduced by any other method of comparison.

It must be with great caution that we proceed to a similar analysis of internal and direct taxes, for not only is it impossible to draw from the treasury reports such satisfactory statements of the manner in which they worked, but the conditions under which they were imposed and collected exposed them to many extraneous influences. Thus, in the first instance, these taxes were subject to fierce political controversy, while, in the second period, they were levied as war taxes and collected under war conditions. They cannot, therefore, be said to have had a fair chance. With regard to these taxes between 1795 and 1801, we find conflicting authority as to the manner in which they worked, but it is

---

[1] Parnell on Financial Reform, p. 122.
[2] Oeuvres de Neckar, tome IV., p. 196.

thought best to rely upon the public statements rather than on the claims of those who made political capital out of the method in which the internal revenue system was managed. The figures, as they appear, are condensed into the following table:

	Total estimated revenue.	Cost of collection.	Moneys rec'd in Treasury.	Estimated rate per cent. cost of collection.	Actual rate per cent. cost of collection.
1795	$ 528,481	$ 84,943	$ 337,755	.15	.25
1796	647,065	88,585	474,289	.13	.19
1797	735,239	86,098	575,491	.11	.15
1798	1,004,828	119,890	644,737	.12	.18
1799	995,000	129,912	779,136	.13	.16
1800	993,661	103,785	806,396	.10	.12
1801	989,533	....	1,048,033	....	....
1814	3,262,197	148,991	1,910,995	....	.078
1815	6,242,503	279,277	4,976,529	....	.056
1816	4,633,799	253,440	5,281,111	....	.048

Notes on the Table.

Of the entire income from internal revenue, the excise on spirits gave rise to nearly three-fifths net receipts.

For first period, compare American State Papers, vol. VII., pages 386, 557, 592, 616, 681, 718, and vol. VIII., p. 18.

For second period, ditto, vol. IX., p. 230.

The first thought suggested by these figures is, that internal taxes are more expensive than customs duties. It would, however, be unsafe to accept the experience of this period as a generalization of wide application, for the cost of collection, as here disclosed, was altogether abnormal, owing to the political environment in which the collection was undertaken. By the present system of internal duties, revenue is collected at an expense of three and six-tenths per cent.,[1] and whenever the

[1] Report of the Commissioner of Internal Revenue for 1882.

two systems have produced the same amount of gross revenue, the advantage inclines to the system of internal duties.

Another notable feature of the foregoing table is the difference in cost of collecting internal duties for the two periods in which they were employed. It is natural to hold the officers, whose duty it was to administer revenue machinery, responsible for its working during the terms of their respective incumbency; but there are several facts throwing light on this discrepancy, which, in addition to breaking somewhat the force of a criticism so adverse to Mr. Wolcott, brings prominently into view certain important facts respecting taxation.

Thus, in the first place, when the amount collected from any form of taxation increases, while the objects taxed remain the same, the ratio of cost of collection to gross revenue will tend to decrease. For example, the receipts of 1816 were six times as great as in 1800, while the cost of collecting the former was but little over twice that of collecting the latter; yet the subjects taxed and the rates imposed were nearly the same in each case. If it be asked why Wolcott did not augment his tax and thus avail himself of this principle, it may be answered that during the two periods the ratio between assessments and amount of national wealth remained nearly constant. The possibility of increased receipts rested upon the actual increase of national wealth and industry, and thus it appears that, other things being equal, cost of collection bears some relation to the ability of a people to pay.

Another explanation of this discrepancy is found in the fact that, during the first period, these taxes were administered in the face of political and party opposition and by a government which did not have at its back a majority of the citizen-electors; but, when the system was again tried, it was by a party popular in all parts of the Union excepting New England, and under such enthusiasm as had been engendered by the entrance of the Nation into war. The first system also was established as a permanent system, while the internal duties of 1813 were specifically called war duties, and it was promised that they should be repealed upon the cessation of hostilities. This fact not only presents a strong apology for Mr. Wolcott, but brings again clearly to our view how important an element is public sentiment in the workings of all revenue systems. The defense offered by the Federalists for maintaining such a system has already been spoken of.

An analysis, however, of the principle upon which the two policies of internal duties were based show, as it appears to me, that Gallatin possessed the financial sense in a higher degree than Wolcott. The error of the latter as a financier seems to have been that he failed to recognize the necessity for fitting his system of taxation to the actual conditions about him. His methods were altogether too artificial. Thus, with regard to the tax at present under consideration, his report of 1796, to which reference has already been made, is most complete as showing the various forms of taxation in the several States, but the only conclusion which he drew from all these facts was, that it was impracticable to harmonize a Federal system with State sentiment and State machinery. When, however, Gallatin came to consider the same question, he did not so conclude, and under his direction there was created an establishment which recognized State-conditions both as regards assessments and collection, and the superior economy of the latter experiment is largely due to this fact. Still, it ought to be said, in justice to the Federalists, that they proposed to create a permanent revenue-organization, while, in the minds of the Democrats, the measure was but a temporary expedient; there was, therefore, more reason in the former case for departing from the established order in the various States.

A study of the administration of direct taxes analogous to the foregoing will not be undertaken. The first direct tax had but a year's trial before the law imposing it was repealed; and, of the two million dollars levied, about seven and a quarter thousand only were paid into the treasury in the course of that year, the remainder coming in driblets during the fourteen years following. The amount actually received previous to 1809, compared with charges of collection as allowed on settlement, shows that the expense of collection amounted to nine per cent. of net receipts.

It will be remembered that during the second period of direct taxation, it was permitted the States to assume and pay directly into the treasury the amounts assigned them, in which case a deduction of fifteen per cent. was made. Seven of the States in 1814, and four in 1815 and 1816 availed themselves of this privilege. In these cases it is perfectly proper to assume the cost of collection to be the allowed deduction, although the rate in other States fell somewhat short of this proportion. From ten to fifteen per cent. may be fairly assumed as the cost of these direct taxes, and whatever may be said for them under more favorable conditions, it must certainly be admitted that, as administered, they were not economical.

It appears, then, from such considerations as have been presented respecting the early forms of taxation, that customs duties were more in harmony with economy of administration than internal duties, whether direct or indirect. It may be that this economy was apparent and not real, but unless the fact be clearly shown, or unless some political reason can be urged for the continuance of an expensive tax, it must fail of defense upon economic grounds. The principle underlying the report of the Committee of Ways and Means, March 2, 1802, which led to the repeal of internal taxes, must be accepted as sound, whether the judgment of the committee be approved or not. This report submitted the opinion that a tax which required one-fifth of the gross amount to bring the remaining four-fifths into the treasury, "can be justified only by an imperious necessity, a necessity which does not at present, and is not hereafter likely to exist."

There is, however, another fact suggested by this comparison between internal and external duties, which finds illustration in the period of revenue history under consideration, and which points to a conclusion somewhat at variance with what has just been stated. Customs duties, it is claimed, are very good in time of peace, but they cannot be relied upon for an emergency. They are not elastic, they do not quickly respond to temporary demands, nor is the ratio between rate and receipts nearly as constant as with internal duties. As bearing upon this claim, it will be remembered that when the second war with Great Britain was undertaken, all customs duties were double; the receipts, however, were not thereby increased. The normal income from duties was about fourteen millions of dollars, but the actual income for the years 1812 to 1816 inclusive, was respectively eight, thirteen, five, seven, and thirty-six millions of dollars. Thus it appears that the doubling of the rate met neither the expectation of Congress in largely increased revenues, nor of the treasury department in keeping the revenue receipts up to the old figures. As it turned out, this seems to have been an ill-advised measure, for it failed to give financial assistance and threw confusion and uncertainty into business affairs. But this is not the full extent of the criticism that may be properly urged against customs duties as the basis of war financiering. The financial policy upon which the war of 1812 was conducted proved an utter failure. It lay in this policy to supply the extraordinary demands of the treasury by employing the credit of the Nation, and to support this credit by throwing the weight of the loans upon the receipts of customs dues. These receipts were neither adequate in amount nor of sufficient certainty to induce confidence, and in consequence public credit quickly and continuously fell, nor did it show any evidence of recovery till liberal laws levying internal taxes had been passed. The fact here disclosed, that customs duties are not adequate to a sudden financial emergency or a long-continued strain, is a truth of general application, and would find corroborating testimony should the history of the financial conduct of the late war be closely scrutinized. An explanation of this is not far to seek. A good revenue system, equal to all demands that may be made upon it, must be elastic, and a tax upon the processes of production, when laid in harmony with financial principles, is always more elastic than a tax upon exchanges. Commerce is more sensitive to external conditions than ordinary production, the margin between success and failure is narrower, and a tax or a war declared will be more quickly reflected in trade than in domestic industries. It is indeed an unwise policy that would rely upon customs duties alone. At least this is the lesson to be gleaned from the financial history of the second war with England.

The question remaining for consideration is quite different in its character from that which has just been reviewed. It concerns industrial history rather than pure finance. The claim is not unfrequently urged by those who are looking on all sides for arguments in favor of protection as a national policy, that the foundation of our early American commerce was laid in 1789 by the discriminating duties imposed in its favor; and also that the rapid extension of domestic manufactures subsequent to 1807 is traceable to the policy of encouragement embodied in the first revenue laws. The question, therefore, for our study is, how far tariff legislation was influential in effecting the establishment of these two industries, and to what extent their development was due to other causes.

The growth of American shipping, from 1789 to 1807, is without parallel in the history of the commercial world. During the years intervening between these two dates, American tonnage, engaged in foreign trade, increased from 127,329 tons to 848,306 tons; that is to say, the capacity of shipping owned by American citizens devoted to the foreign trade had increased six and eight-tenths times. No one claims that this growth was proportional to the extension of domestic industry and agriculture. Normal tonnage is sometimes estimated as the amount required by a people to carry half their exported and imported commodities while foreign peoples are permitted the same privilege. This is, perhaps, an arbitrary estimate, for the carrying service, like the service rendered in manufacturing and agricultural pursuits, should be subjected to the guidance of the principle of division of national labor, that is, it should be open to the rulings of international competition. Still, for purpose of illustration, this form of calculation may perhaps be accepted, and upon the basis of this test, in order to prove that registered tonnage in the United States in 1807 was normal, it would be necessary to show that every inhabitant produced exportable commodities to the amount of seven-tenths of a ton. This could not have been the case under the industrial conditions of that period. We may, therefore, conclude that the shipping business of the time was properly termed the "carrying trade."

It is a peculiar fact that the observed fluctuations of the American carrying trade, previous to 1807, follow closely upon the important political events in Europe. That is to say, the commerce of this country discloses a peculiar sensitiveness to diplomatic moves on the part of the great belligerents then struggling for mastery on the Continent. There is then presented the possibility of finding in the peculiar condition of the Western world at this time, and in the fact that the United States was the only important neutral power, a full explanation of the surprising extension of American shipping. The principal diplomatic events pertaining to commercial affairs have already been mentioned in connection with the tonnage acts. It will be sufficient, therefore, at this time to draw attention to the control which they seem to have exercised upon trade statistics of this country. For the sake of greater clearness as well as greater conciseness, I have endeavored to present this relation in tabular form, and in such a manner that the entire argument may be shown at once to the eye. Upon the left, arranged in chronological order, may be found a statement of the political and diplomatic events to which reference is made. The first column of figures shows the total exports of the country; the second and third show the exports of domestic and foreign origin respectively. This division of exports does not appear in the public records previous to 1803; the figures previous to that date are estimates. The fourth column shows the pounds of sugar annually exported, this

Year.	Political and diplomatic events.
1791	....
1792	....
1793	Treaty of the Allied Powers....................
1794	Jay treaty negotiated with England....................
1795	....
1796	....
1797	French cruisers allowed to capture American vessels for any cause recognized as lawful ground of capture by British treaty.........
1798	Order in council granting "special indulgence" to American shipping. French treaty declared void by United States and merchantmen allowed to arm....................
1799	....
1800	....
1801	....
1802	Treaty of Amiens, followed by reënforcement of the Colonial policy by Great Britain....................
1803	European hostilities renewed, followed by relaxation of Colonial policy. Order in council not to molest trade with French colonies.
1804	....
1805	....
1806	Berlin decrees issued, American vessels trading in British goods threatened....................
1807	(*a*) Jay treaty expires. (*b*) Monroe treaty rejected. (*c*) British orders in council issued, requiring license to trade with Europe. (*d*) Interpretation of Berlin decree making it effective against America. (*e*) Milan decree issued, denationalizing ships submitting to British order. (*f*) Congress lays embargo on all American shipping....................
1808	British orders repealed as applied to Spain....................
1809	Embargo repealed by Congress, June 28....................
1810	....
1811	....
1812	War declared with Great Britain by American Congress, June 18..
1813	....
1814	....

commodity being selected because it is of foreign origin, and thus shows distinctly the importance of the neutral position held by this government. By bringing goods under the protection of the neutral flag of the United States, freight and insurance was much reduced. Alexander Baring estimated the advantages which the American trader could offer to the West India exporter to be twenty-five per cent. over that which could be offered by the traders of any other country.[1]

Total exports.	Exports of domestic origin.	Exports of foreign origin.	Pounds of sugar exported.	Revenue from customs and tonnage.
$ 19,012,000	....	....	74,000	$ 6,873,783
20,753,000	....	....	1,176,000	5,095,919
26,109,000	....	....	4,439,000	6,720,985
33,026,000	....	....	20,721,000	8,671,195
47,989,000	....	....	21,377,000	11,253,733
67,064,000	....	....	34,848,000	12,681,866
56,850,000	....	....	38,366,000	13,001,105
61,527,000	....	....	51,703,000	11,528,091
78,665,000	$35,000,000	$43,665,000	78,821,000	15,439,569
70,971,000	35,000,000	35,971,000	56,432,000	16,181,425
94,115,000	40,000,000	54,115,000	97,565,000	20,828,240
72,483,000	40,000,000	32,482,000	61,061,000	15,150,428
55,800,000	42,205,000	13,594,000	23,223,000	14,528,652
77,699,000	41,467,000	36,231,000	74,964,000	20,799,635
95,566,000	42,387,000	53,179,000	123,031,000	23,897,664
101,536,000	41,253,000	60,283,000	145,839,000	26,538,987
108,343,000	48,699,000	59,643,000	143,136,000	27,323,277
22,430,000	9,433,000	12,997,000	28,974,000	11,348,694
52,203,000	31,405,000	20,797,000	45,248,000	11,843,576
66,757,000	42,336,000	24,391,000	47,038,000	16,898,539
61,316,000	45,294,000	16,022,000	18,381,000	10,660,666
38,527,000	30,032,000	8,495,000	13,927,000	13,300,910
27,855,000	25,008,000	2,847,000	7,347,000	7,965,568
6,927,000	6,782,000	145,000	*less than this.*	4,806,022

The fifth column presents the receipts to the public treasury from customs and tonnage.

[1] Inquiries into the Cause and Consequences of the British Orders in Council, p. 37.

In a study of this table, allowance must be made for tardiness with which news was transmitted at that early day. The facts to be observed are the following. In 1791, there began those disturbances which threw all Europe into commotion. On account of the policy adopted by the Allied Powers, a policy reciprocated by the French, the carrying trade of the European States was greatly embarrassed. It was, however, essential to the welfare of the colonies, as well as for the interest of the governments at home, that some means should be provided for the exchange of European and colonial products. In general, we may say this was accomplished by making use of the only important neutral power, the United States. This was the safest method that could be devised, although it necessitated the adoption of a somewhat circuitous route. The first part of the journey, from the colonies to a port of the United States, was by permission or acquiescence of the European Power; the second part, that between this country and Europe, was upon the basis of treaty. In both stages of the voyage, commodities received the protection of a neutral flag. This was the basis of the trade carried on in American bottoms between England and her West India possessions. The Jay treaty, it will be remembered, as first presented, secured direct trade but prohibited traffic with British colonies. This particular article, however, was rejected by the American Congress, which resulted in leaving that trade subject to the control of the King and council. The consequence was, that, so long as it was England's interest to have her goods carried by American ships, commodities, the products of those Islands, were carried in the manner described. This power of the council was not exercised to the hindrance of trade until 1801, at the time of the first peace, but upon the renewal of hostilities, trade fell again into the old channels and so continued till the expiration of the Jay treaty in 1807. The figures that the best illustrate this commerce are those found in the column showing the number of pounds of sugar exported.

The events of 1807 put an end to this lucrative trade. The naval condition of England on the one hand and the determination of Napoleon to have no neutrals and to destroy English trade on the other, deprived the United States of her peculiar advantages hitherto enjoyed, while the retaliatory measures of the home-government destroyed whatever opportunity for commerce there was remaining. It is no cause for surprise, therefore, to notice that trade of all kinds fell off in 1808. In view of such facts as these, it seems that one cannot reasonably impute the great increase of American tonnage between 1789 and 1807 to the discrimination made by our laws in favor of home-shipping. These regulations may have placed this country, for the time, on a par with foreign nations, so as to have secured to her a share in her own carrying trade, which she otherwise would not have enjoyed, or they may have permitted her to see, more quickly than she otherwise would have done, the importance of being the only great neutral power in the Western world; but to say that this discriminating policy was the cause of the growth of American commerce during the period we are considering, is to burden a very weak cause with an enormous consequence.

Turning now our attention to the establishment of the textile industries, we shall find the causal factors yet more complicated than was the case in the development of shipping. There are three sets of facts that, in an exhaustive discussion, ought to be taken into consideration: (1) the revolution in methods of manufacture occasioned by the invention of new machinery and its introduction into this country; (2) foreign commercial complications already alluded to, which forced all capital and energy that could be spared from agriculture into shipping, thus precluding its employment in manufactures; and (3) the tariffs imposed for "protection and encouragement" of these industries.

But first let us learn the facts respecting the development of the textile industries. It is believed that no violence will be done the argument if our search extend no farther than the establishment of the manufacture of cotton goods. There were some few attempts to carry on the cotton industry in this country at quite an early period, but the first successful endeavor that brought into use the newly invented methods, seems to have been in 1790, in Pawtucket, Rhode Island. This was under the management of Samuel Slater, a man well acquainted with English machinery, having been previously an employee in the Arkwright factories. Through him machinery was introduced and instruction in its use given to those who desired it. Still there was no important development in this industry for a number of years. In 1803 there were but four factories in the country. Yet it appears that attention was about this time drawn to the possibilities of this business, for during the next four years there were established eleven additional mills. The development of the cotton industry, however, cannot be said to have begun till 1808, and from that time till 1820 it was very rapid and, on the whole, successful. According to the report of a special committee made in 1816, the development of the industry, as shown by the number of factories and their capacity, was as follows:

	Number of Factories.	Number of Spindles.
1801	62	31,000
1811	87	80,000
1816		500,000

The number of spindles here given for 1816 is an estimate, and probably an exaggerated one; still, the report is as important for our purposes as though it were perfectly accurate, since it not only shows a rapid development during the four years of the war, but indicates also the excessive views of the importance of cotton manufactories at that time, and explains the willingness with which protection was granted to them in the revision of the tariff in 1816.

Without entering further into details, the truth regarding this industry is, that, previously to 1816, the tariff had no potency in effecting its establishment or maintenance. The energy and capital of this country flowed in the channel of least resistance, or, what amounts to the same thing, followed the greatest inducements. Previously to 1807, the neutral carrying trade absorbed all surplus energy, but this field of activity having been closed by the diplomatic events of that year, and later all trade having been cut off by the declaration of commercial war, the capital and labor, freed from its accustomed employment, undertook a new form of industry. In 1807 there may be discovered, operating as a permanent cause, that which in 1803 gave temporary direction to the investments of capital. It was the destruction of the carrying trade that occasioned the establishment of manufactures in this country; the potency of the tariff was very slight. If further proof of this were desired, it would only be necessary to compare the rate imposed before the United States were cut off from the European market, and the rate conceived as necessary to maintain these industries thus abnormally developed after the return of peace again permitted importations. The former was fifteen per cent.; the latter was twenty-five per cent. upon a minimum price of twenty-five cents per yard.

From the play of forces here presented there are one or two lessons that may be advantageously drawn. The one is, that there is here enforced, by a chapter of industrial history, a doctrine of capital sometimes lost sight of in discussions upon the policy of protection, namely: National industries are limited by national capital. Its converse, also, may profitably be noticed, that, given capital and labor freed from industries already in existence, new enterprises will be undertaken. Of especial pertinence is this to the United States at the present time. In a country that produces raw material and food supply, the growth of commerce and manufactures are proportional only to a very limited extent. Intensity in the one necessitates a languishing condition in the other. From 1793 to 1807, trade was brisk, and this country lived from foreign supply, growing rich all the time because the people possessed energy and thrift; from 1807 till 1816, trade was supplanted by manufactures, and people depended upon home-supply, growing rich during this period also because they possessed energy and thrift. But, with all the tariff-laws and tonnage-acts that have been passed from that time to this, they could not have undertaken both pursuits during both periods. For the first twenty-five years of our national history, extensive commerce meant languishing manufactures, and extensive manufactures meant languishing trade: both could not exist in their highest vigor. It is as logical for a Protectionist to depreciate trade, as for one who believes in Freedom of Production to insist upon the benefits of the principle of division of labor.

The financial history of the United States points with peculiar emphasis to one fact, and that is the danger of employing a power granted for one purpose for a purpose entirely different. In the discussions upon the first revenue law, Mr. Clymer of Pennsylvania, one of the few men who saw the tendency of the language employed, desired a separation of the bill into two parts; one of which should contemplate revenue alone and be shaped entirely by revenue principles. This suggestion was not, however, favorably accepted; and as a consequence, there was included in the first finance bill, in addition to provisions for securing a revenue, part of the country's navigation laws and the major part of its formulated foreign policy. Although, as has been shown, the distinctively protective character of revenue acts does not make its appearance till much later, it yet remains true that a precedent for using revenue machinery in a loose manner was then established, and out of this precedent have grown many of the abuses which subsequent history discloses.

Looked at from this point of view, one may hold the first Congress responsible for the dangers that threatened the country in 1831, for the disasters that followed the distribution scheme of 1836, and for the absurd position in which the people of the United States now find themselves,—with an overflowing treasury and yet unable to shut down the floodgates of revenue. The financial reform which this day requires is more than a modification in tariff-rates; it consists rather in such a revolution of public sentiment that finance laws may be judged on the basis of financial principles, and revenue-machinery be employed primarily, if not solely, for revenue-purposes. If the disturbing element of protection can in this manner be separated from questions of finance, the injustice and expense of paying a subsidy out of public funds for the support of losing industries will clearly manifest itself. Tariff-reform means tariff for revenue only.

Made in United States
Troutdale, OR
11/03/2026

56844427R00046